Where Is Your Boat Headed?

Igniting the entrepreneurial spark for those eager to live life on their terms.

TANYA DODARO

FriesenPress

One Printers Way
Altona, MB R0G 0B0
Canada

www.friesenpress.com

Copyright © 2024 by Tanya Dodaro
First Edition — 2024

All rights reserved.

No part of this publication may be reproduced in any form, or by any means, electronic or mechanical, including photocopying, recording, or any information browsing, storage, or retrieval system, without permission in writing from FriesenPress.

ISBN
978-1-03-918635-4 (Hardcover)
978-1-03-918634-7 (Paperback)
978-1-03-918636-1 (eBook)

1. BUSINESS & ECONOMICS, WOMEN IN BUSINESS

Distributed to the trade by The Ingram Book Company

Dedication:

To a man who, while on earth, always encouraged me to confidently determine the destination of my boat. From heaven, he continues to guide me through the wind at my sail.

My late father, *Dennis Grujich*.

Lea and Cara,

May the winds be kind, the storms be short, the seas clear and blue, leading you to discover your own islands full of treasures you could only dream of.

FOREWORD:
THE PATH TO WONDERMENT

In a wild moment in an environment filled with overwhelm—while in the middle of reading emails, helping the kids with homework, making dinner, with major project deadlines coming up and halfway through creating a new business plan—I find myself asking, why am I so keen to take on this book project right now? During such a busy time in my life, it's something that would end up being more involved and time-consuming than any other project I can ever remember working on. The answer came quite easily.

It is necessary; a must; it is my calling.

I needed to carry out this project specifically for those who are in the exact same position that I found myself in once upon a time. The crossroads. A moment in your life that is faced at some point by every single entrepreneur that ever lived, where the wind is blowing from every direction and noise is coming from everywhere. You are drowning in a mix of emotions where fear and excitement are one, and out of this moment of madness, these questions demand an answer: Which road do I take next? Do I stay on course? Or do I move forward into the unknown?

From a distance, one road looks smooth, freshly paved, and has a sense of calm. The birds are chirping, and the sun is shining; it feels familiar and comfortable. The other road seems bumpier, maybe a little cool and misty, there is a fearful feeling of what dangers might lay ahead. It's uncomfortable; just looking at this road gives a similar sense to dipping your toes in freezing cold water. But past this, far into the distance, there is a strange sentiment of curiosity and wonder about what might be waiting at the end of this unfamiliar road. The attraction to this road is without reason, but rather there's an intense and unexplainable force that is gently whispering in the wind and nudging you with persistence. Deep down, your heart pulls you toward this path, knowing it will be uphill and with rain clouds, but the desire is too strong to deny. You decide to take the first step.

The crossroads is a familiar situation faced by all the women featured in this book.

When looking at our stories, it's no surprise that we all chose the path of wonderment.

The stories you will read speak of those that place value on building their own empire of greatness, are driven to succeed amidst failure, and who focus on living life according to the terms they create.

This book is designed and written by and for entrepreneurial women. It is a call to women who might be standing at their own crossroads and thinking about following their own path to wonderment.

I chose to take a unique approach to writing a book about entrepreneurship by curating a wonderfully diverse group of women from across industries, with unique backgrounds, experiences, and perspectives, with the one commonality of them all being successful female entrepreneurs. My desire is to bring deeper value and meaning by featuring the stories of multiple women in hopes that you will see yourself through some of the beautiful stories of success that you will read. Each chapter represents one theme that will bring tremendous insight as you get ready to take the path of most resistance with the hopes of uncovering gifts with values that are amazingly unquantifiable.

The analogy of an ocean to entrepreneurship is dear to my heart, and it gives me so much pleasure to share this with the outside world. It gives me a sense of nostalgia and reminds me of my childhood. I was raised by two parents who were entrepreneurs. My father's motivation was ignited through talks given by some of the best speakers at the time; he would listen to them often, especially on cassette while in the car. He would frequently play them for my brother and I when we were in the car, in hopes that something would stick. Little did he know that decades later, this infusion would be the inspiration for not only this book but for my entire career, life path, and a focus for how I raise my two daughters. His favourite was Earl Nightingale, and we would listen to him on repeat. One part of his audio program from *The Strangest Secret* always rose to the top for me, and it has been a driving force. So much so that I named my book based on this concept: *Where Is Your Boat Headed?*

FOREWORD: THE PATH TO WONDERMENT

> "Think of a ship with the complete voyage mapped out and planned. The captain and crew know exactly where the ship is going and how long it will take and it has a definite goal. And 9,999 times out of 10,000, it will get there.
>
> Now let's take another ship and just like the first and only let's not put a crew on it, or a captain at the helm. Let's give it no aiming point, no goal, and no destination. We just start the engines and let it go. I think you'll agree that if it gets out of the harbor at all, it will either sink or wind up on some deserted beach as a derelict. It can't go anyplace because it has no destination and no guidance."
>
> – Earl Nightingale

If only my late father could know the impact of his determination to lead his children toward a path of entrepreneurship. His efforts inspired a thirst for higher success and helped us to remove the idea of barriers from our minds.

I faced my first crossroads at twenty-five years old. I took myself out to lunch one day to design the life I wanted to live, and I have been living it ever since. By creating this book, I hope to motivate and spark other women to do the same. Let us model a positive relationship with entrepreneurship for those who are thinking of taking the leap. I hope you enjoy this forever project of mine: to inspire and advocate for budding entrepreneurs everywhere.

CHAPTER 1:
THE CAPTAIN

Success.

There are probably numerous images flashing through your mind as you read this inherently powerful word.

Doing what you love?
Shutting down your computer at 3:00 p.m. every day?
More money?
Spending more time with your kids?
Being more present in your life?
Vacationing abroad?
Retiring early?
Finding a fulfilling career?

Every single one of these mental pictures can represent success, and there's no such thing as a right or wrong answer.

Do you know why?

Because success means different things to different people. To the same person, it also means different things at different stages of life. Our definition of success when we're fifteen isn't our definition of success when we're twenty-five, forty, or sixty-five.

CHAPTER 1: THE CAPTAIN

State of mind, perspective, life experiences, and present goals all play important roles in how we choose to define success at any given point in time.

Today. Right now. This very moment. What is *your* idea of success?

....

Nice to meet you, I'm Tanya.

Woman.
Entrepreneur.
Married to my high school sweetheart.
Mother of two girls.
Lives in Toronto, Canada.
Impulsive risk-taker.
Hard worker.
Identifier of challenges.
Deviser of killer solutions.

Two steps forward, one step back. That's how the saying goes. Except that in this case, it was more like ten steps back.

Here is a snapshot of my August 2012:

1. We moved homes.
2. I was a new mother of two — nursing my six-month-old baby, mothering my three-year-old — and managing the juggle of home and work life.
3. My mother took a turn for the worse and wound up in the hospital indefinitely.
4. My business partner (pregnant with twins) was vacationing overseas, so On Q Communications (the

company we founded in 2005) was all in my hands and it was a very busy time for us.

5. I was one of the primary caregivers for my mother and my aging grandmother. In other words, my life consisted of nonstop running around, going from home to home, in and out of the hospital, to and from the office. Kids or no kids, I had no choice but to be where I was needed.

6. In what felt like no time, I suffered the blow of indescribable heartbreak when my mom passed away.

7. The new On Q Communications office was under renovation. All staff members were temporarily working out of my business partner's basement, which then flooded, displacing everyone (keep in mind this was before work from home was commonplace).

My business partner's delivery date was approaching quickly. Even though this was supposed to be my maternity leave, there was no choice but to get back to business.

It was too much.

Life had reached an unprecedented level of difficulty, and I knew I had to find a better way.

As I drove my older daughter to Montessori school one morning, the entrepreneurial wheels in my head began to turn.

Driving is wasting a lot of my day.

My daughter loves her school, and especially her teacher.

Her Montessori teacher had confided in me that she is looking for a leadership role.

CHAPTER 1: THE CAPTAIN

Good childcare centres are all waitlisted in the area.

There's a vacant unit in our new office building.

I could hire my daughter's favourite teacher to lead, open a childcare centre, and it would be a solution for other families in the area and those who work for On Q Communications.

I could have my children attend preschool in the same building as my office.

It would save time on drop-offs and commutes.

I would have a say in the programs and education that my kids receive.

Might this be the perfect solution?!

Excitement began to bubble up within me. I was onto something.

The next step was to see what others thought of the idea.

My brother thought I was positively crazy. What did I know about starting a childcare centre? Not to mention the fact that I was already a business owner and a mother of two young children.

My business partner never thought my idea was unreasonable, but mentally, she simply wasn't there yet. Her twin babies were still on the way, and all of us mothers can most certainly agree that it's a whole different ball game once our little ones come into the world. Being pregnant is a vacation in comparison to the wonderful chaos that your life becomes starting on birthing day.

Mark, my husband, understands that once I've set my heart on something, there's no turning back. At the same time, his support for my endeavors remains a constant I can always rely on.

Truth be told, others' doubts don't particularly faze me. In fact, I believe they fuel me to investigate my ideas further. I always know that I am the captain of my own ship.

The more I thought about my idea, the more sense it made. Without dropping the ball on my business, without letting go of the things I cherished most in my life, I had created a solution to regain that important balance we all strive for, but seldom get.

Leveraging my impulsive nature, I realized it was time to put the plan into motion.

We called it Bizzy Bees. I developed a business model that made the centre both attainable and feasible. Bizzy Bees was an answer to what had become a complicated life matter. There simply wasn't enough time in a day, and I knew life could be different. I just needed to figure it out.

The model was quite simple. Fees would be competitive yet lower than other centres' and the teacher would receive a good salary. After factoring in all costs and tweaking the model, I realized my own children could attend for free. Given the fact that another preschool for two children would run me a considerable amount, this was great!

Don't get me wrong, launching a childcare centre wasn't easy in the least. I knew absolutely nothing about the business. I vividly remember looking through countless educational catalogues and frantically jotting down notes on a piece of paper in the early planning stages and thinking to myself, *What am I doing?* From licensing, to hiring, to meal programs, to developing curricula, it was a complex endeavour. Within five months, we were up and running. Bizzy Bees then ran itself quite independently and I became totally hands off. The staff I hired was absolutely instrumental in the success of the business, which is yet another testament to what you've likely heard many times before: *hire the right people.*

Looking back, I think opening Bizzy Bees was one of the best things I did for my family and business at that time. My aha moment that day when I was dropping my daughter off at the centre, combined with the development, launch, and operation of Bizzy Bees taught me what my idea of success is: *being able to have it all, just the way you want it.*

By having it all, I don't mean the money, the car, the husband, the kids, and the house. I'm talking about balance and the ability to be exactly who, what, where, and when you want to be. It's a totally different mindset to say you want life on your terms. You are not focused on managing your circumstances; instead, you are busy creating them.

I like to think of success as a puzzle. In order to have it all, I need to fit the puzzle pieces together tightly, perfectly, and beautifully. This might mean changing the design of the puzzle in order to adjust and adapt to life's ebbs and flows. Every new corner I turn or hill I climb has the potential to alter my puzzle, and I'm prepared for that and willing to put in the work to make sure the pieces always fit. I make *my own* decisions in order to design *my own* life.

The term *entrepreneurship* often stirs up thoughts of wealthy, busy workaholics. I find the media sensationalizes entrepreneurship and defines what success should look like by creating stereotypes. I've even spoken to female entrepreneurs who bluntly say, "Oh, I never took a mat leave; I'm a business owner." Since when did being a business owner mean that you were automatically denied the opportunity to fully immerse yourself in motherhood for as long as you felt you needed?

Success and this notion of having it all directs us to challenge old ideas and traditions. It's time to relook at the entrepreneurial paradigm. And it begins with a changed mindset. A mindset that is fundamentally characterized by a belief that there are no constraints, no limits on me, no barricades that prevent me from doing what I believe I need to do to be successful, and most of all, allows me to be happy.

Success is being fulfilled in every facet of life, as much as possible. Success is subjective. It's personal. It's different things to different people at different times. Figure out what it is for you and shape your life around that notion.

I've had to reconfigure my forever puzzle many times throughout the years … but as captain of our own ship, that's what we do best.

From Me to You:

Success is balance, making things work for you,
by designing it as you want it to be.

– **Tanya**

CHAPTER 1: THE CAPTAIN

A Tale from the Sea

Keka DasGupta
Founder of Precision Marketing Group Inc.
and The Art of Life-ing with Keka

As women, some of us are attracted to the entrepreneurial path for practical reasons — to provide for our families, seek freedom, be our own bosses, or fill an important gap we see in the marketplace or society. For others, we jump in because we feel called to do something bigger. We follow a dream. We pursue a vision. We dive into a passion. Even if everything isn't clear at first, we know it's something we *must* do. Sometimes our entrepreneurial pursuits are a mix of these motivators, and at other times, we simply fall into this journey by happenstance (unless you believe, like me, that everything happens for a reason!). No matter what brought you here, I want to congratulate you for trusting yourself and listening to your instincts. You are giving yourself permission to pursue your dreams. This reflects self-belief. Keep betting on your success!

I've been an entrepreneur for sixteen years now, and I can tell you, choosing this pathway can mean you are about to embark on the most exhilarating journey of your life. It can give you autonomy, purpose, meaning, and impact at heights you would never have previously imagined possible. This is where you can truly live life on your own terms.

But here's the catch: I've learned that along this voyage, success never unfolds in a straight line. This route is characteristically squiggly. It is messy. It is unpredictable, filled with unexpected twists, turns, and blind spots. Plus, when you are the captain of your own ship, maintaining control over your entire journey alone can feel lonely. There is no "boss" to revert to when challenges surface. You *are* the boss. As the saying goes, "The buck stops with you." So, in this chapter, I'm going to share three foundational insights that I use as anchors in navigating my businesses. Consider the numerous navigational instruments a captain has at her disposal, such as a magnetic compass, radar, echo sounder, GPS receiver, etc. If her instruments fail her, however, she can still use a fool-proof method for steering her ship to her desired destination: She can navigate the ocean using the stars in the night sky. This ancient art of celestial navigation has been guiding seafarers for centuries.[1]

Similarly, we can learn to trust the knowledge inside of us, using the external signs and signals that the universe provides. These are important reminders of the validity of our entrepreneurial missions. After all, entrepreneurship is where great ideas come to life and change the world.

To this end, please allow me to share Two Truths and a Lie (well, more accurately, Two Truths and a Lesson). I routinely revisit these insights when I need to *return to me*—to trust myself when facing business adversities.

Truth #1: Remember, your idea found you!

Along your journey, especially if you are birthing *never-been-done-before* ideas as an entrepreneur, know that not everyone will see potential in your concepts as you do. Naysayers—even well-meaning ones—may question your choices and beliefs.

---

[1] https://www.formulaboats.com/blog/navigate-using-stars/

CHAPTER 1: THE CAPTAIN

Don't let them steer you into abandoning ship. As captain, you always have over-riding authority.

Trust yourself.

Why? Because your entrepreneurial idea found you. It chose you. A dear friend and fellow female entrepreneur, Lesli Ferguson, founder of the powerhouse design firm LikeLike Studio, told me this once. And this insight has been by my side ever since.

I was excitedly sharing with Lesli how the idea of "life-ing" came to me one night to denote the idea of *doing* life on purpose and on our own terms. It's a word that I just made up to best reflect what I was thinking. That is when Lesli said: "Oh Keka, your idea has found you!" This is how she sees it: There are many ideas out in the universe that need carriers. When they find the right person to deliver that message to the world, a perfect match is made.

Whenever I have a "Who am I do to this work?" moment or a "How dare I dream that big?" moment — common self-limiting and self-doubting thoughts that creep into the minds of many entrepreneurs — I simply re-shift my focus. I have a responsibility to bring this to the world. This idea is bigger than me, but it chose me to deliver it. I *get* to do this work. How lucky am I? This helps me trust myself again, recognizing that I am the right person for this calling, and as such, I can do this! Obstacles are only temporary until we find solutions around them.

Never let go of the fact that your entrepreneurial idea found you and you can turn it into something bigger than yourself.

Truth #2: Your idea's mere existence in your head means the universe can make it possible

In entrepreneurship, we often start with an idea that may seem brilliant to us, but there is no existing way to execute on it. We must build that road from scratch. This can be easier said than done, and it's another common breeding ground where self-doubt and self-limiting beliefs fester.

I was listening to Oprah and Deepak Chopra on Super Soul Sunday, and their discussion focused on the notion that if an idea comes to us, that fact alone means the universe can make it possible. In other words: An idea's mere existence already confirms its viability. The net takeaway is that we must subscribe to our own dreams. Don't say "no" to yourself before anyone else does. Trust yourself, trust your ideas, and trust your actions because your entrepreneurial dream IS possible in some form and manner. Once we've done everything we can, we must surrender the results to the universe and let things unfold as they are meant to unfold.

Imagine how you would feel if you knew that even when things looked uncertain, everything you were working towards WAS possible? How would that knowing give you confidence in yourself and your entrepreneurial work? How would trusting yourself and, as a result, trusting your destiny completely change the way you approach your challenges?

And finally, the lie: Gratitude letters gone wrong?

Affirmations often show up as quiet whispers to prove to us that the universe is betting on our success.

CHAPTER 1: THE CAPTAIN

This lesson completely changed how I approach my speaking business, The Art of Life-ing with Keka (this work today feels like it's my soul's mission in this life).

To illustrate the lesson, please allow me to take you back to a school auditorium just one month before the global pandemic shut down life as we knew it for more than two years.

....

Booming laughter fills the air. I can feel my cheeks are flush. There are 250 students in the auditorium, all ranging from grades six to eight. I look over at the teachers standing against the side and back walls. They look mortified. They are helpless to do anything due to their union's work-to-rule mandate.

Standing at the front of the stage, I'm reluctantly realizing that as a professional speaker, I have completely lost control of the room. I'm embarrassed and disappointed in myself. That inner critic in me — that little voice inside — is harshly judging me.

I didn't see this coming. I had delivered this keynote to over 10,000 students in-person, and this had never happened before.

As I'd always done, near the end of my presentation, I asked students to write a letter of gratitude to someone important in their lives. In my experience, eighty per cent of the time, without prompts, children write that thank-you letter to their parents. Another fifteen per cent of the time, they write their note to their teacher. Once they complete their writing, I usually ask if any students want to volunteer to come up on stage to share their letter with their peers. This has always been a powerful, moving exercise that resonates with young students.

Not that day.

Everything was going well until one young boy came up to the front and decided it would be funny to talk about how he was grateful to himself because he didn't kill his little brother that morning for being super annoying. His words prompted a chain reaction, and other students started begging me to share their letters too, only to come up on stage and make fun of others to entertain their peers.

My program, called "Gratitude Mirrors," which was designed to promote bullying prevention using gratitude, kindness, and empathy, felt more like a crude comedy festival. I quickly ended my presentation and dismissed the students.

I started packing up my audio-visual equipment as students packed their bags and left the auditorium. All my insecurities, doubts, and fears that I had pushed aside when I first embarked upon this entrepreneurial work were flooding back to me. This was my last presentation of the day. I'd already conducted four back-to-back keynotes at that school. The principal had been so excited to bring me in after seeing my work online. I felt like I had let her down too.

Let's face it. I'm a PR and marketing professional. That's what I've done for two and a half decades. What makes me think I can possibly parlay any of that work into mental wellness and anti-bullying? Just look at what happened in this last presentation! Who am I to do this work anyway? I have a degree in psychology, not education. I don't deserve to call myself a professional speaker.

As the proverbial question of *worthiness* dominated my thoughts, I was interrupted gently by two young girls standing in front of me with the warmest smiles on their faces. They were each holding papers that they reached out to give me. Speaking for both of them, one of the girls said, "We just wanted to say thank you so much for your presentation today. It was awesome. We both wrote our letters *to you* and wanted you to have them. Here you go."

Of all the scenarios I could have dreamt up in that moment, this would not have been one of them. I was so touched! I couldn't help but reciprocate their smiles. As I reached my hand out to accept their letters, they thanked me once again and gleefully walked away. I stopped everything I was doing and looked down at the letters.

....

The first letter read:

Dear Keka,

I want to thank you for teaching me how to look at people from different perspectives and how to give gratitude towards others.

You've taught me that sometimes people are mean to each other, but it's not because they want to be. It's actually because people were mean to them, and they just passed it on. I also learned that I should live in the present, and whatever happened before, happened, and I can't change that.

Please keep doing what you are doing and teach others about their gratitude.

Kind regards,
Crystal

P.S. You're beautiful, and I mean it.

....

The second letter read:

Dear Keka,

Thank you for sharing this presentation with me. You showed me how to show gratitude to others and how different people have different perspectives. I now know how to make someone's day become one of the best days, thanks to you. The presentation you made also made my day better in many ways. I feel like the girl in the picture with great joy in this moment!

Best wishes,
Emily

....

Truly, I was awe-struck.

The girls' letters not only mirrored back to me the exact messages I was trying to relay from my keynote, but their words of encouragement to keep doing what I was doing felt like a message from a higher dimension. I took it as a gift from the universe.

Suddenly, that "Who are you to do this work" voice in my head that had been getting louder and louder fizzled away. Almost effortlessly, these young girls' heartfelt words negated any worries that my content was not strong enough to have an impact. These letters were proof of its power.

I started to recall now all the times in the past when students had approached me post-presentation to say, "You changed my life." When I first heard those four words, they were so powerful that I didn't know how to fully accept them deep inside of me. It was easier to say, "Aww, these kids are so sweet," and leave things at that.

Now, I was reminded that I needed to honour the intent with which those students shared their kind and supportive words with me. All of this recalibrated my perspective, bringing me back to the fact that this is my soul's work.

The protectionist fear function that we all have inside of ourselves can often mis-read or over-exaggerate the data flooding our psyche in precarious conditions. It can lie to us. It can over-amplify negative cues and downplay, or even miss, the positive affirmations that feel like whispers sent our way.

The letters from those two girls felt like proof points to me that the universe is indeed betting on my success. It has my back.

This experience also reminded me that as entrepreneurs, we get to define what success means to us. Experience has taught me that I can't expect to deeply resonate with 100 per cent of my audience, 100 per cent of the time. But if each time I speak, I can change even one child's outlook at a foundational level so that positive impact stays with them for the rest of their lives, then I have succeeded. I want to do that every day for the rest of my life!

As the captain of my own ship, I recognize that I know myself better than anyone else. I will never let someone else convince me otherwise — even if that someone else is the negative voice inside my head, desperately trying to protect me from anything other than the status quo that it knows so well.

I trust myself above all others because I am the captain of my own ship.

As you embark upon your entrepreneurial journey, I invite you to do the same.

From Me to You:

Subscribe to your own dreams because the universe is betting on your success.

– Keka

CHAPTER 2:

THE ENGINE

The engine. The word alone holds such a strong energy. When you think about where your boat is headed, it's the engine, the horsepower, the driving force needed to propel things forward that is at the absolute beginning of any journey. It is the most powerful part of the boat; without it, it would never be able leave the dock. Once you start the engine, you know the boat will move with strength and vigour. It will push past waves and almost anything that comes into its way. Unlike boats that ignite with a turn of a key, our true power is found within the depths of our minds.

We all have desires in life, but a dream without action is only a wish. Action is our engine; it is what makes us leave our dock every day.

Once our engine is running and we set sail on a journey toward realizing our dreams, it's usually a path that winds, goes uphill and down, straightens and bends. The scenery around us may change as time passes, and we're never absolutely positive what lies ahead. The engine just keeps pushing forward.

What is it that decides our path? Is it all up to us? Is it destined to be one way or another? Is it nature or nurture, or both? Does one decision shape our path, or many? How much does our upbringing have to do with it? Our childhood? Education? Friend choices?

The answers differ according to who you're talking to. Maybe you think you've been in complete control, taking the driver's seat all the way along your path. Or perhaps you feel that you haven't had much of a say in where you've ended up.

Each of our lives is as different as is the path that guides us.

My journey has often veered from a traditional path.

On one such occasion, when I was graduating from elementary school in grade six, I was honoured with the position of valedictorian. While I was preparing my speech, I decided that I would ask each student in the class to dress up in a way that portrayed who they would be and what career they would have years later. As my big graduation day quickly approached, I spent many hours trying to decide on the career *I* would dress up as. I hadn't realized that it was such a great proposition to my classmates until I acknowledged the soul-searching activity it precipitated within myself.

I pondered and thought hard, frantically going through all the most common careers my friends chose. None resonated with me.

Teacher? Patience isn't my strong suit.
Veterinarian? NO, I'm allergic to dander!
Doctor? No, that's quite a bit of schooling.
Accountant? More math, no thank you!

CHAPTER 2: THE ENGINE

Nothing of what many of my classmates shared with me prior to the big day got me excited in the slightest. So, what then? Just a few days before my graduation, my lightbulb moment came. My parents were watching the six o'clock news and I asked them, "What is the name of the career of that person who is speaking on TV?"

They answered, "A journalist."

I proudly went into my graduation wearing a suit and holding a briefcase with the letters "CBC" taped to the front. Most classmates had no idea what I was, but I didn't care, I stood proud, now knowing where my boat was headed. I was totally content going against the grain in my decision.

A foreshadow. Little did I know back then that I would wind up pursuing a career in journalism, and even further, majoring in broadcast *and* landing a job with on-air presence! Was the law of attraction at play? I will leave that to you to decide!

When I was young, I recall closely observing my parents in their daily lives. No matter the season or the year, they always made their own schedules and prioritized what was important to them, including running successful businesses. My father wouldn't start his day until saw us off to school—yes, very unorthodox for men back then. His favourite was sitting at the kitchen table first thing in the morning, sipping his coffee and reading the newspaper while my brother and I ate our breakfast before school. As he read, he was "directly" teaching us about world events, but was also "indirectly" teaching us that he was the designer of his own life and he was living it on his terms.

You know those things that happen and you don't appreciate them at the time, but then they come to mean so much more later on? My day of appreciation came when I was twenty-five.

I had just lost my father, and I was sitting down to write his eulogy. In it, I spoke of his personality, all the characteristics people loved him for, and how much I adored him, but there was something in particular that I had inadvertently come to hold so dear to my heart. That very thing just so happened to speak volumes to the kind of man he was and what he stood for.

Throughout all the years I lived with my family, while in school and even afterward, there was never a single day in my life that my father did not walk me out of the house and wave to me until I was completely out of sight, whether I was leaving on foot or by car. I know this because I would often turn around just to make sure, and there he always was, with a smile and a wave. Rushing out of the house to "punch-in" at 9:00 a.m. was never part of his day. He made a point of designing his entire life, and I was witness to it. I now find I do the same with my daughters every single day. The fact that I make a point of doing this means much more than my unwavering commitment to show up — it's my way of carrying on his legacy by modelling living life on my terms.

My father's career was in the world of real estate development and the locations of several of his projects were outside the city. He would often take long drives to his project sites, and I would accompany him. Truth be told, he'd need to twist my arm pretty good to join him, since playing with my dolls was far more exciting at the time. But he was very persuasive, and I would always gladly end up being his sidekick. I'm grateful I was because now I realize that I learned some of my best life lessons on those drives.

On one particularly long drive with my father, I remember asking him if he was happy with his career and he answered, "If someone offered me a full-time job as an employee with an annual salary that paid me double what I make now, I would not be interested." At such a young age, I didn't entirely understand the depth of his response, but I knew his answer intrigued me tremendously because he said it with such confidence. This marked the first moment of my life that I began to wonder about entrepreneurship, what it meant to him, and what it could possibly mean for me.

Ever since I was a little girl and for as long as I can remember, entrepreneurship has been running through my veins.

Choosing to go out on your own, and I will even go so far as to say "going against the grain" on your career path as an entrepreneur is a tough decision. It's accepting an unknown path, having confidence in your own abilities, getting excited about the potential that lies ahead, self-motivating at every corner and picking yourself up at every wrong turn. And all the while, it's knowing that the second you make the decision to say "yes" to entrepreneurship, you put yourself in control of your own destiny. This is a very powerful feeling that can't be matched by much in life.

Say it slowly: "Live life on your terms."

Think about the possibilities! Doesn't it sound almost magical? Don't be fooled, however, because making the decision to be an entrepreneur and actually arriving at this decisive point, takes *a lot* of time, energy, and deep thought.

I consider this the before period where you whip your mind into shape for that big day when you are finally ready to say "yes!". It's like a daily commitment to get to the gym, pick up your twenty-pound weights, and rep it out.

Do you have a business idea that will solve a problem or fill a need?

Have you come up with a solid execution plan?

Who is your target market?

How will you reach out to the masses and let them know about your idea?

What about financing?

How will you keep motivated even when things get impossible?

The what's and how's are popping up everywhere!

University and college courses teach us the necessity of business plans, competitor analysis, marketing strategy, balance sheet forecasts, and income statement projections. The academic lessons we learn about business are specific and formulated.

The thing is, that's not real life.

While it's a good idea to appreciate and understand the value of these teachings, it's also important to let them go. To realize that business life is unique, fluid, and constantly evolving. A good business owner doesn't always follow the rules they learned in school; rather, he or she adapts to the situation. It isn't about doing it a certain way — it's about doing it the way that works for *you* and *your business*.

I often find it insightful to observe my daughters. They will hear someone talking about a fun business idea and very soon after, they will come up with a business idea of their own. They don't hesitate, they are ready to go the moment they have their big idea. They don't worry about the rest; they just know they will figure it out. Cara recently decided to open a handmade jewellery business, selling through Etsy and at markets. With very *little* thought and *a lot* of beading, she was able to turn a

CHAPTER 2: THE ENGINE

profit. Sometimes as adults we can become tainted by negative experiences and overthinking. We would have found twenty reasons why it wouldn't have been a good idea, but I find my girls teach me things every day, more than I could have imagined.

When we train ourselves to let go of the rigidity and embrace the unknown, we open the doors to everything that *is* possible. We allow ourselves the trust and confidence to figure it out. To make it work. To succeed … whatever that looks like.

My father bought me a plaque when I was very young, and I put it up in my room by the door. It said: **Tough times don't last, tough people do.** Throughout my childhood, it stayed on my wall, just above my light switch; I saw it every time I walked in and out of my room. Its wisdom has been a guiding force throughout my life.

When you own a business, success and failure become one, and only the tough will survive. It should be expected that success and failure are the yin and the yang to the point where you almost can't separate them. The failure machine fuels the success machine and sometimes, vice versa.

My grandmother, who was one of my very best friends, would always tell me that life is like train tracks, where the good and the bad run in parallel, throughout all your years. It's important to recognize challenges, but also savor the joys at the same time. This analogy has been a valuable lesson for me as a business owner.

Now back to my own workout analogy. You finally get ready to say "yes" to entrepreneurship, after repping out your weights enough times that your muscles are positively popping, your mind is now ready and you've gained the inner strength to move forward. For many, this is the scariest step. Unless you make the choice to not be afraid of it.

When I was sixteen, I decided I wanted to go skydiving. I had no fear and nothing stopping me mentally or physically. It was just something that I really wanted to do. With some decisions in life, you must approach them like you did when you were sixteen, with that same childlike, carefree mind.

Just jump!

Everything else will fall into place.

From Me to You:

Do you want it? Is the only question you need to answer; don't worry about how or when. Just answer the question.

– Tanya

CHAPTER 2: THE ENGINE

A Tale from the Sea

Richa Gupta
President & Founder, GOOD FOOD
FOR GOOD & Turmeric Teas

Boats can have different types of engines—inboard, outboard, stern drive, or jet drive. While some engines power and steer, others propel and direct. Whatever the boat and whatever the engine, one thing remains constant: the engine drives the boat. Without it you can hover or sail; however, motoring through the waters ahead is impossible.

It wasn't until I was in my thirties that I realized I was the engine of my own boat and my own life. Propelling my boat forward wasn't always easy, nor was it clear which way to steer. But through both light and dark waters, there is one thing I never failed to do as the engine of my boat: drive.

Listen to the Voice

Ever since I was a teenager, fashion was all I wanted to do. You'd think I would have been happy, sitting in the corporate offices of Hudson's Bay as a fashion buyer.

I wasn't. The little voice in my head was sublimely dissatisfied. I had spent more than a decade in the fashion industry in three different countries, and here I was, questioning my future.

While it is always honest and wise, that little voice we have in our heads only takes us so far. It tends to highlight the dissonance in our present situation, but doesn't show us the path to take, nor does it offer any kind of solution to remove that dissonance it senses so strongly. It only leaves us feeling uneasy, uncomfortable, and unhappy.

My dissonance was deeply rooted in the fundamental nature of the fashion industry. I found it to be vain and superficial, and I longed for something with meaning—something that could make a real difference.

As a new immigrant to Canada, transitioning into another field wasn't going to be easy. Knowing very well that education would be a great investment in myself no matter what, I shifted into the world of academics, where I also hoped to find my true calling.

I turned my boat around and propelled it in a different direction to enroll in the master's program at the Schulich School of Business in Toronto. During my studies, a new industry began to capture my interest: food. I convinced myself that everyone needs food and it's a basic necessity that isn't superficial, like fashion. Perhaps I could make a difference in the food sector and the little voice in my head would be at peace.

My post-MBA career began at General Mills in marketing. This was it! I had made it! This was a career that would pay my bills and give my soul the satisfaction it needed.

To no avail.

It *did* pay my bills, so easily in fact that I was also able to enjoy the luxuries of life including a nice car, high-quality clothes, toys for my daughter, and entertaining outings whenever we felt like it. But my soul was empty.

From the outside, I had achieved success. On the inside, the little voice in my head had become louder than ever.

My job led me to discover all the additives and preservatives that went into processed food, none of which have anything to do with nutrition. The name of the game was prioritizing taste and convenience over health, driving up product consumption instead of nutritional value, and replacing ingredients to make the food cheaper or longer-lasting on the shelves.

Dissonance had returned to my life. This time, it was exceedingly difficult to switch directions because I found myself in golden handcuffs, locked in a career that paid so well, yet left me so unfulfilled.

Create, Don't Wait

> **"The best way to predict your future is to create it."**
> —Abraham Lincoln

I was a young mom and a busy marketing executive trying to climb up the never-ending corporate ladder. It was a lifestyle that left me constantly feeling guilty about not being able to cook fresh, wholesome food for my only child. Everywhere I looked for shortcuts I found food products loaded with harmful ingredients.

That's when a new idea struck me. What if I could create and sell food that would make it easy for people to eat healthy and at the same time make food accessible to those who couldn't afford it? What if I could build my own social enterprise?

This idea propelled me to unlock my golden handcuffs, and again, leave what many would describe as an incredible job, so that I could try to satisfy that relentless little voice in my head. It wasn't easy, but my engine was also relentless and now I was free to steer my boat toward calm waters.

Once this new idea came to me, I simply had to give it a try. Good Food For Good was born, and it was like falling in love! Since then, I've played a major role in pioneering the Better-for-All Food Movement. Consumers are offered a "better" food product in the sense that it is made using only natural ingredients, it gives back to people in need, it's environmentally friendly, and it's beneficial for society.

All Good Food For Good products are free from CRAP (**C**hemicals, **R**efined sugar and artificial sweeteners, **A**llergens, **P**esticides), delicious, convenient, and packaged in sustainable glass bottles. With every purchase, we donate money to feed a person in need — a unique model in the food industry that I call "Buy One, Feed One." I knew I was making a difference when two things happened:

1) busy moms like me chose Good Food For Good to prepare a tasty meal without the guilt of feeding their families unhealthy food, and

2) our food bank partners were able to feed thousands of people through our Buy One, Feed One program. Every inch of my body could sense that I was on the right path, and it's what made me continuously push forward, regardless of the challenges I was faced with. And many a challenge there was.

I went from high-paying mental work to performing physical labour that paid nothing. I was a one-woman show, with 5:00 a.m. wakeups, sourcing, cooking, packaging, and then carrying heavy boxes of sauces from the trunk of my car to the table at whatever local food market I'd found for that day. It was extremely hard work and long hours, but I was feeding my soul.

Even though I was no stranger to the food industry, this work was very different from what I'd done previously. I went from being part of a large team in consumer packaged goods to being a solopreneur. At General Mills, if I needed something, all I ever had to do was email my team. They had the required technical expertise to complete the task, and my job was done. In this new role, I had to be the leader *and* the team member. My learning curve didn't have a curve anymore. And as for my engine, I was asking for all the power it could give me. I revved onward through the water.

When it came to product research and development, there was no swaying me from my vision to create sauces and condiments using only the ingredients people use at home. Everything had to be organic and free from preservatives. Outsourcing to highly experienced R & D specialists in the industry was out of the question because they only knew how to create products using specific lab-made additives. I was all alone, pressing forward through choppy waters with no calm in sight.

Shelf life, supply chain management, and consumer demand were just a few of the issues that plagued Good Food For Good.

If I made my products without any preservatives, how long would they last on store shelves? Would stores buy them? Without any points of comparison or best practices to follow, for many months I tested, week after week, to ensure my products were okay for consumption without any preservatives.

My commitment to wholesome, organic ingredients greatly impacted the time it took to bring the products to market, and it was extremely difficult to source organic ingredients at the right quantities and prices, particularly dates and spices.

Sure, *I* cared about real, wholesome food, but I didn't know if there were enough people who shared that value with me. Local farmers' markets gave me the real, face-to-face consumer feedback I needed. It was backbreaking work, from making the sauces to transporting the product to standing behind a table for hours, just hoping people would find value in what I was creating.

In the beginning, turning a profit was out of the question. I wasn't taking home a salary because my commitment to giving back started on day one. I wasn't going to compromise my values for corporate profits—not ever. And some years, that meant giving back more than I was earning.

But I was building something meaningful.
I was creating the future I had always dreamed of.
And the little voice in my head was finally happy … and quiet.

Purpose Brings Peace

For the first time in my life, I felt at peace despite the fact that I was making very little money, spending countless hours away from my family, and doing very "uncool" things like packing boxes and cooking for obscene amounts of time. And that's how I knew I was really on to something.

If I could feel genuinely happy, fulfilled, and peaceful even though my work encompassed all these seemingly less-than-desirable factors, maybe it was desirable for *me*. Maybe I'd finally found my meaning in life. Perhaps this was my purpose—the purpose I'd spent so many years trying to discover.

My engine kept my boat pressing on through all kinds of waters, only now, it wasn't to remove dissonance from my life, it was to propel forward toward the realization of all my dreams. My engine drove me to grow and expand my purpose so that it would have even greater meaning in my life, and the lives of others.

At General Mills, I used to get a headache every day. Now, I can't remember the last time I had one. My back used to be so sore, I couldn't go for more than four weeks without a massage and my therapist would tell me my body felt like I did physical labour (meanwhile I sat at a desk all day long). Today, much of my work is, in fact, physical labour, and yet I have no back pain and haven't needed a massage in years. And my skin cleared up — it's never been so good in all my life. When we are deeply stressed or unsatisfied, the repercussions of this state not only manifest in our minds, but also our bodies.

If we understand this, then we can also see that our minds and bodies are capable of telling us when we are not on the right path. The question is, are we ready to listen? Are we open to identifying the dissonance? And can we muster up the courage to change directions? When we are not happy about the day's journey, it's time for introspection. We must allow our thoughts to come to the surface so they may serve and guide us toward what we truly deserve in this life: *finding our sense of purpose.*

From Me to You:

We can only ever truly be happy if we find fulfillment in what we do.
The little voice in your head is there for a reason. Listen to it, follow, it and let it guide you toward the discovery of your true purpose.

– Richa

CHAPTER 3:
THE WAKE

From the minute you said "yes" to entrepreneurship, all the possibilities and excitement for what's to come consume your thoughts every minute of every day. You have a burning desire to go, go, go! Everything you see or hear fits into your almost-obsessive focus on business, and it can be overwhelming at times. You're at a point where all you think about is how to make it work. You have a chance to make a difference and leave your mark on this Earth.

The beginning of entrepreneurship is the most meaningful. It's early enough that you haven't been tainted with the hardships of business life, and all you see is rainbows and lush green fields ahead. And that makes this the very best time to *just charge ahead!*

As you move forward in your business planning, remember that it doesn't have to be a lonely journey. One of the best strategies I implemented early on was to create an environment where I was supported by impactful mentors who helped guide me. I believe strongly that the key to success is surrounding yourself with professionals, and people you look up to who can give you that irreplaceable support. You need a team to help you balance your ideas, keep you grounded, lift you up, and help you move in the right direction at any given time. Plus, it's always great when you can avoid learning by trial and error!

When it comes time for you to reach out to someone who has the potential to become a mentor to you, ask yourself these questions:

Whom do I admire and respect?

Whom do I trust?

Whom do I love spending time with?

Who has walked a path that I strive to reach?

What key characteristics do they have that I need in order to be my best business self?

Early on in my business path, I was blessed with mentors who were authentic and supportive, and it made all the difference. In the beginning especially, when there is so much doubt and so many obstacles present themselves, having strong support is vital.

For me, there has always been one exceptional mentor, someone I've consistently look to for advice and guidance. She is a remarkable woman I've long admired, and among the most successful individuals I've had the privilege of knowing. It's an incredible feeling to have someone truly believe in you, as it fosters self-belief. Nearly two decades ago, when I first shared my aspiration to start a business, she embraced the idea. Her 'think big' philosophy has been a guiding principle in all my decision-making. Just knowing I had someone in my corner, passionately supporting my success, made everything feel attainable.

It's important to look for a mentor who has similar ideals as you, and who makes it obvious that they have a genuine desire to see you become a success. Always strive for growth and improvement—aim to find someone whose expertise complements your strengths and surpasses your experience.

While they're not exactly mentors (although you'll probably find they can come pretty close at times), it's important that you make the effort to get your family members on board with your vision. Your partner, your kids, your parents—whomever it might be. These are the people you come home to every day, share your best and worst moments with, and naturally turn to for advice. Having supportive partnerships is what gives you that extra fire power when you need it most.

When I initially made the decision to start a business, I chose to embark on an entrepreneurial journey alongside my friend. This choice was not made lightly; it involved careful consideration. Choosing a business partner is much like finding a life partner. The ideal business partner is someone you'd regard as one of your very best friends. There will be occasions when you spend even more time with your business partner than your spouse. Recognize the significance of this decision and draw the parallel. It's a crucial choice that can tip the scales between success and failure.

Remember those early days of learning to ride a bicycle on two wheels? You needed some support, and there was that initial wobble and uncertainty. But once you found your balance, you were off! Now all there was left to do was keep your head up and pedal. The same goes for the start of your business: once you're up, it's go time! Day after day, new challenges will arise, but that's the fun of it. Just keep pedalling.

One of the initial hurdles most business owners face is acquiring new clients, a concern that weighs heavily on everyone's mind. A practical approach begins with common-sense strategies: connect with colleagues, participate in networking events, harness the power of social media, and, above all, spread the word about your business among your personal and professional contacts! They alone can be a goldmine.

I'll forever cherish the moment when we secured the first significant client with my first business venture. The setting was Boston, Massachusetts. The task ahead was huge, but we were committed and prepared to seize any opportunity that came our way. With flying out of our budget at the time, we embarked on a ten-hour drive to Boston to present our proposal in response to a substantial RFP (Request for Proposal) from a US corporation. We were fuelled by hope and determination. In the weeks leading up to this pivotal event, we were dedicated to meticulously crafting a comprehensive forty-page proposal to clinch the deal.

And we did. And it was a big win!

En route to Boston, I vividly recall the mix of nervous excitement. But on the journey back, I felt like I had won a big prize. This feeling of victory had little to do with monetary gain; it was a testament to the sheer effort I had poured into a goal, and through hard work, I achieved it. It was a moment of pure joy, and I could feel it deep inside me. I couldn't help but cry, scream, and laugh all at once. The celebrations in Boston that weekend were unforgettable.

With each future client win, our confidence grew, fueling our determination to build upon our successes. We were not only prepared to continue on our path to success but also eager to take on new challenges and extend the boundaries of our accomplishments. This momentum instilled in us the belief that with every step forward, we were not only gaining ground but also empowering ourselves to reach even greater heights.

Whenever I have a day when motivation is hard to come by, I pause for a moment and transport myself back to that winning moment in Boston. Just recalling the relentless determination I had on that day instantly revitalizes me. This strong memory is one of the key reasons why I'm a firm believer in journaling. Keeping a record of your experiences with intricate details is valuable. It allows you to revisit those moments and relive them, as we all understand that nothing quite compares to the magic of the first time.

Take a moment to consider yourself and your company. When aiming to attract clients or customers, it's vital to accurately define your target audience. Who is interested in what you offer? How will you reach this specific market and create awareness of your presence? Understand your role in their decision-making process. Keep your requests to potential clients and customers straightforward, and avoid getting lost in the specifics. Trust your instincts, but also seek counsel from mentors and loved ones to back your decisions.

Looking back, I realize I didn't have it all figured out in the beginning. Quite the contrary. The first client signed on before we even had a formal corporation or an office! However, the sequence of events didn't affect the excellence of the service we delivered. What truly matters is how you perform at each step, not the order of events. You're not expected to have everything perfectly set up from the start. In fact, having it all pristine and perfect would rob you of the thrill of being an entrepreneur.

Over the years, many things have evolved, but one constant has remained: attitude. It has consistently revolved around a singular theme—I'm committed 100 percent and will do whatever it takes to find solutions.

Finding solutions refers to navigating the daily challenges that demand creativity, finesse, strategy, and insight. If you're fueled by drive, motivation, and determination, this problem-solving ability emerges instinctively. Because you persist. You advance, leaving an ever-expanding trail of impact—your wake.

From Me to You:

Journal your journey. Keep notes, jot down your feelings, sensations, emotions, and the valuable lessons you learn along with powerful experiences. These moments are unique and will never return, but your journal entries offer a gateway to relive them. Plus, you never know when they'll provide the spark to rekindle your motivation one day.

– Tanya

A Tale from the Sea

Livia Grujich
Owner and Speaker, Prescribing Happiness

The wake is the wave a boat generates as it moves through the water. The energy invested in the creation of this wave is never diminished or lost. It will propel through the water, impacting all and creating ripple effects through and through.

....

If you were to look back at my childhood, you would have never guessed I'd end up an entrepreneur.

My mom was a chemist, and my dad was an engineer. Both were very smart, determined individuals, each with a good education and superior work ethic. They taught me the value of hard work, and were always making sure that I was on the right path so I could get a stable, well-paying job and provide for my family.

I was a good kid.
I listened to my parents.
I did well in school and appeared to be precisely on the path they wanted for me.

Consistently on the honour roll, naturally I had my pick of universities. After much deliberation, I wound up attending one of the country's top business schools. This is what prepared me for a great nine-to-five job. Sure enough, following my graduation, I landed the nine-to-five of my dreams!

So then, why oh why, when all the signs were pointing in the complete opposite direction, did I know deep down that I wanted to do "my own thing"?

In my recent dig-up of things past, I came across an independent study project from my university days. The subject matter: *work-life balance*. What did I know about this way back then? What intrigued me enough to *want* to know more about it when I was twenty years old? And why did I place such a high level of importance on it that I chose to dedicate a whole semester to its intricate study? So many years later, I can tell you that one of the aspects of entrepreneurship I value most is the control it gives me over my work and my life, and most importantly, balancing the two.

Right out of university, my dream job enabled me to be independent and set my own hours. I thrived! I remember thinking to myself, *Why would I want to be in an office with a boss telling me what to do when I'm so good at setting my own goals, planning my whole day on my terms, and reaching my targets?* I thought I was the luckiest person in the world to have the sales job everyone else wants. That is, until the day I was speaking with my boyfriend (now husband), and he said, "If I had your job, I wouldn't wake up in the morning."

I realized it at once.
The fact that my personal discipline is what allowed me to have freedom in my career.

As I consider my work choices over the years, it is clear to me that it was the freedom I always sought.

There I was. A successful career woman with what I considered to be the greatest job, working for a large multinational company. And yet, I always knew I wanted my own business.

Why did I value that so much?

Maybe because I considered it to be the ultimate freedom. Running your own company is what enables you to decide what you do, who your clients are, who you work with, when you take vacation, when you take mat leave, how much money you want to make, what time you work, and what time you see family.

Interestingly enough, I never questioned why these things were important to me until I found myself sitting here, writing this very chapter. I simply figured that everyone values these things, and if you're disciplined enough and you have the drive to work hard, you get to have them.

Throughout the years when I did in fact have my own company, I learned quite the opposite. Not everyone does value these things. Some people prefer stability. About five years into growing our company, we made the decision to offer one of our employees a significant promotion, one that would give her much more autonomy and, well, freedom. We couldn't have been more excited to offer it to her. The meeting day arrived and we sat together and presented her with the offer. She denied it. Quite simply, she explained, "Thank you, but I don't want that. I like the structure of my nine-to-five job here and I need people telling me what to do and when to do it."

We were stunned.

Like the nine-to-five structure?!
Need people delegating?!
Huh?!

Why didn't *I* need or want these things? If you look at my two biggest role models, the dynamic duo I admire and love, does it not make logical sense that I would have followed in their footsteps? I was always the girl who looked up to my parents, listened to what they asked of me, valued their guidance and opinions, and wanted to please them.

So you can imagine how I felt on the day that I announced to them that I was quitting my "wonderful, stable job" at the "big, stable company."

I'll never forget our conversation. I believe their exact words were, "But, why? You have a great salary. And a car. And a job in a large company with room to grow. Great benefits! And a pension! And all the granola bars in the world!" They were speechless.

My boss, on the other hand, completely understood when I handed him the resignation letter. He told me outright that he knew all along I wouldn't be around forever. He said, "Some are lifers here, and for others this is just a stepping stone."

There's no doubt about the fact that this was, indeed, my dream job. There was just one problem: it was still a *job*. I wanted more. I wanted to make a difference in the world, to do the work I chose to do with the clients I chose to collaborate with—and all on my own terms completely. I believed in myself and I knew I could do it. My attitude was, *What's the worst that can happen? If I fail (and I won't—that's never an option), I can always re-enter the workforce and get a job.*

This may have been the first time in my life I went against my parents' advice. And I don't think they realized it at the time, or maybe ever, but their choices and sacrifices are what ultimately enabled me to reach the place where I am today.

They grew up in a communist country. My dad was an engineer (and a math teacher!). He is the smartest man I know. He can hold a conversation on just about any topic under the sun, from physics to soccer to the capital city of a tiny country you've never heard of on the other side of the world. He's the life of a party (though he'd insist he's an introvert!). He has a huge heart, and anyone who knows him feels his warmth. My mom was a chief chemist. Talented and dedicated. She runs the show. She's in command and in control. But to me she was Mama: my mentor, my friend, my go-to. She always made sure my brother and I had everything we needed. She instilled confidence in us by always reminding us that we're the best!

Growing up, you never put too much consideration into what your parents do for a living; you just know they go to work and they pick you up from school. But as you grow up, you start to wonder and to explore and to consider what your calling may be. Your parents' choices, their way of living, and the way they raised you, ultimately influences who you are and how you lead your life.

I had been in conversations with my mom about the fact that I wanted to do more with my life, how I wanted to make a real difference, and how I didn't know what my next step should be to get there. She answered by saying, "I wish I could give you advice, but we never had these questions. We knew if we studied science in university, we would get a job in the city. That was our goal, so that's what we did."

In their home country, my parents were constrained. That beautiful, overzealous childhood question of "what do I want to be when I grow up?" was dictated by the government, which limited what you could be in order to lead a life that let you supply for your family. You were told how much time you were permitted to take off to have a child (one month!). My parents made the best of it and provided for my brother and me in every way possible. Nevertheless, the conversations and stories we've heard throughout our lives have always centred around them wanting to be able to give their kids more. The "more" they spoke of is something they knew existed, whether it was in a time before communism, or in another place altogether. It was this longing to give us more that led them to flee. They left everything behind — their parents, their families, their childhood memories, a country and language they loved — all to be able to provide more for their children.

Up until very recently, I didn't know what "more" really meant when they spoke of it. But as I look back with an observant, analytical, and understanding lens, I now see. "More" meant "freedom" — the ultimate gift for their children.

We think we're so different from one another. I think it of them. They think it of me. Stable job income earners versus insecure career status entrepreneur. But that's only what's on the surface. A deep dive into the core, defining lifetime goals and aspirations of each of us, and it's clear as day. We were after the same thing: *freedom*. I quit the job of a lifetime to go out on a limb, accept the risk, and follow my heart in order to have freedom in my career and in the way I lived my life. They dropped everything and took the biggest risk imaginable to immigrate to a new country so they could attain true freedom in their lives and those of their children.

I cannot fathom the sacrifice they made, starting over in a new country with nothing. When they first arrived in Canada, they had no money and no home, they didn't know the language, and had to accept jobs they were overqualified for — all for the ability to give my brother and me the choices and liberties they never had. It's impossible for me to repay them, even though nothing would give me greater pleasure. My parents taught me that a child never repays or thanks their parents, because a parent doesn't need that. As parents, we do the best we can with what we have in order to make our kids happy. That's part of the "parent code" that every parent innately understands.

I never questioned why I always knew I wanted to be my own boss, or why I placed such high value on work-life balance. I did, however, know with certainty that I would not bend or accept any role that didn't allow me to have both. Through self-reflection as a parent myself, I have pieced the puzzle together. Every choice I make is with my kids in mind. The same way as I myself am the product of parents who were determined to achieve more for their kids.

They succeeded.
And so did I.

Our paths aren't so different after all.

From Me to You:

Don't ride the wave. Be the energy that creates it!

– **Livia**

CHAPTER 4:
THE COMPASS

As women, our hearts often guide us, and whether this is agreeable to some or not, it holds true in many ways. The reality is that most of the decisions I've made, decisions led by my heart, have been the ones I never regretted.

Each of us possesses an inherent compass known as intuition. In ancient times, it safeguarded us from predators and helped us find food. Today, we trust our intuition to steer us toward sound life choices, aiming for an improved and fulfilling life.

Intuition is a subtle force; it rarely shouts its wisdom. Often, it's just a faint, quiet voice, easy to miss if you're not paying attention. It doesn't help that we live in a time period where the noise of the world is deafening. We can't imagine life without multitasking, we have our phone in one hand, a child in the other, while we are typing on our laptops with our toes (or at least so it seems). Social media is now an integral part of our daily routine, even in our professional lives. Media has consumed us between pandemics, wars, and racism. Technology is ever-present. Our constant connectivity is altering our behavior and thoughts. We're frequently influenced through texts, emails, and direct messages more than we'd care to admit. Remember asking a friend for dinner ideas? Perhaps you've texted a photo of your outfit to a friend to ensure it's suitable for an upcoming wedding. Have you ever dined at a recently discovered restaurant solely because of its reviews? It can even extend to texting a question to your partner who's in the same house but on a different floor! It's a never-ending cycle, and at times, it can be ridiculous.

In many cases, we may not even be aware of how external factors shape our decisions. Intuition, that quiet inner voice, often gets drowned out by the bombardment of constant interference around us. Recognizing this is a significant step. Intuition exists within us for a purpose, an innate guide in our human psyche.

I've launched several businesses, and with each new venture, I had to face various challenges. External influences can be quite hard to ignore, from alarming news about a potential recession to outdated stereotypes about women in business. Even well-meaning friends and family, while caring, often make unsupportive remarks like, 'Why invest your time in this?' or 'It's already been done before,' or the classic, 'Why work so hard?'

Each time, I try to turn to my inner compass for guidance. Of course, it's not without its share of sleepless nights filled with self-doubt, but it has consistently steered me in the right direction. When I overlook it, it almost shouts, 'I've been here all along; why aren't you listening to me?' Amid the constant noise in my surroundings, when I'm faced with a significant decision, I make a conscious effort to spotlight that quiet inner voice, giving it the stage it deserves. In the end, it's like a mic drop moment, and I simply listen.

We discover that our intuition is seldom mistaken. Think of it as a free, built-in tool that stands ready to guide you whenever you require it. Focus on it, heed its advice, and leverage its power. It's available to all of us; we just need to learn how to tap into it when the need arises.

I was dropping off my daughters at school one fall morning when I witnessed the most fascinating sight. Their school is situated near a valley, close to a river, and the campus is full of animals and nature. After we said our goodbyes, I turned the car around, only to hit the brakes quickly. I saw something you don't see every day: a large flock of ducks crossing the street, maybe twenty of them! What was interesting was that the pack of ducks looked to be comprised entirely of adult ducks, but then buried right in the middle of the pack were four or five tiny baby ducks. The scene would have captured the heart of even the toughest onlooker. What was so fascinating to me was that the baby ducks were strategically positioned right in the middle of the adult ducks. It was a perfectly symmetrical shape, with a seemingly equal number of ducks on each side. Nature can be most amazing when you stop to appreciate it. How did the ducks know to position the little ones in the middle and huddle around them while crossing a dangerous street? It seems that this flock of ducks had a strong intuition that led them to safety. How nature can reflect human life is marvelous.

Immediately, a metaphor caught my attention. The adult ducks displayed their wisdom by strategically positioning the most vulnerable members, shielding them from the outside world. In much the same way, as humans, we often safeguard our most delicate thoughts from the world. We don't want them to be discovered by others; instead, we keep them tucked away, where they won't be seen. Consequently, they end up getting buried, like the baby ducks, in the middle of more dominant thoughts that surround them. In many instances, we even forget about them because they remain silent unless disturbed or revisited. The truth is, these thoughts can hold profound significance in our lives and have the potential to spark breakthroughs.

Frequently, these thoughts can be a wellspring of creativity and innovation, offering a source of fresh ideas, ingenious solutions, and even the motivation to push forward. Rather than keeping these thoughts hidden away or dismissing them, it's often more fruitful to explore and embrace them. Think of your thoughts as the delicate baby ducks, each one with the potential to evolve into something remarkable if given the proper care and attention. By nurturing and allowing them to grow, you open doors to a world of possibilities, and you may be surprised by what these initial inklings can become when they are encouraged and allowed to develop.

In the journey of life, we each hold a unique path. Regardless of whether you subscribe to the notion that life unfolds according to a predetermined plan or that you have full ability to shape your every step, both perspectives are inherently remarkable and both have a guiding compass at the helm to chart your course.

Life's journey, whether planned or spontaneous, is bound to present its fair share of trials and tribulations. It is in these moments of darkness, when the world seems uncertain and the path unclear, that your determination shines brightest. Just as the stars have guided sailors through treacherous waters for centuries, your compass will guide you like the North Star through even the darkest waters.

From Me to You:

Keep an eye out for synchronicities, those subtle signs that seem to align effortlessly. It's not a conscious effort; you're naturally drawn to them. Have faith that the universe is orchestrating your path towards success.

– Tanya

CHAPTER 4: THE COMPASS

A Tale from the Sea

Ana Gabriela Juarez
President, CTA Environmental Consultants
Founder, Women in Mining Central America
President, A2J Minerals
Non-Executive Director, Royal Road Minerals

Imagine you are out on the open water, in the middle of the Atlantic Ocean. You've gone a little too far and now you're in over your head, without any sense of direction. You're lost. Right, left, forward, back, north or south — your next move is unclear. The vastness of your surroundings reminds you how small you are, and while the scenery is stunningly picturesque, you still need to figure out where to go.

When it comes to this, there's only one solution: *listen to your inner compass.*

....

A compass is defined as an instrument that indicates direction. Our inner compass refers to instinct, intuition, and that powerful gut feeling that tends to be inexplicable, yet often right. The thing about following your inner compass is that every move you make is a leap of faith. Since there's no data, no science, no research, and no written proof for what you feel inside of you, every decision you make on those grounds is one whose result is entirely unknown. Each step is up to you. Either follow your inner compass, or you don't.

In my life, the concept of gut instinct came from my parents. For as long as I can remember, I've been watching the two of them take leaps of faith in their professional and personal lives. When

I was two years old, I moved with my family from my homeland Guatemala to Germany, where my father was completing his PhD. We didn't have any family or friends there, nor did we know the language, but my parents had a clear objective in mind and a growth plan for our family. Now, as entrepreneurs and founders of several companies including CTA Environmental Consultants, a global environmental consulting company in the mining and energy sector, my parents have taught me that you cannot always look at the statistics when you're building a company or setting a plan for your life. There won't always be concrete information to back up your decisions. On the contrary, if you have a strong feeling that you ought to do something — anything — then, you must do it.

In the world of entrepreneurship, you don't start from money. You don't have success and affluence right from the beginning. Therefore, everything you do has to come from your gut, your internal compass. While this is true, the second part is seizing that critical feeling. You might have a countless number of gut feelings in your lifetime, but it takes time and experience to recognize them and decide to act. You must believe, push forward, and go after what you are visualizing that does not yet exist.

From a young age, I understood the fact that in order to work at the family company, I needed to study in the environmental field. When I was eighteen, I took my own first leap of faith. While I was determined to further my education, I was at a loss as to how, where, and in which program. I packed my bags and followed my inner compass unquestionably back to Germany to take part in an internship. With no idea how everything would unfold, there I was. I didn't know whether or not this move would assist in my acceptance to university or if it would get me any closer to my higher education goals, but I chose to trust my decision. I sensed this was where I needed to be

CHAPTER 4: THE COMPASS

and the rest would follow. And it did. I earned my bachelor's degree in environmental sciences at the Humboldt University of Berlin, after which my master's degree took place in England, where I also met my partner. Degrees in hand, we moved back to Guatemala, and soon after, had our son.

Beginning at age fourteen, I grew up in the family business and became actively involved as soon as it launched. At first, the company was run from our home, where I would answer the phones, deliver packages, and distribute Christmas presents during my school holidays. The business grew quickly and within seven years, there were more than fifty full-time employees. Today, we have four offices in North, South, and Central America, and we are working on projects in more than eighteen countries spanning three continents. Taking on numerous roles, over the years I have worked my way up from field assistant to president of the Canadian office, which required my family and me to immigrate to Canada in 2017.

Opening the Canadian office of CTA was a significant inner compass decision. We are one of the only companies in our industry to come from Latin America, and only the second Guatemalan company to open an office in Canada. While many companies operate the other way around (expand from Canada to Latin America), it does not typically happen the way we did it. And that required us to take a leap of faith.

As a Christian, my inner compass is strongly associated with my faith, and I have found that the two go hand in hand. They co-exist and co-function in my life. First, I listen to my gut. Then, I pray and call upon God to reaffirm that strong internal feeling. Before I choose my next move, and particularly if the path before me is not crystal clear, it is my faith that confirms what I have ultimately decided is, in fact, the right way or the wrong way.

When we opened the CTA office in Canada, we knew it was a risk, but we chose to take the leap. Everyone told us how difficult it would be, what a long and arduous process was ahead of us, and how long it would take to be fully set up. The funny thing is, it was anything but. Every way we turned and with each new task we performed, doors were opened, opportunities were presented to us, and the procedure was quick and simple. No barricades, no roadblocks, no crazy hoops to jump through. It just *worked*. And before we knew it, we were open and ready for Canadian business.

The decision was our inner compass.

The seamless process was God's way of telling us we were indeed on the right path.

When we're trusting our inner compass, even though we may doubt the path and look for the odd confirmation here and there, we're not expecting downright failure or adverse outcomes. Most of us, quite simply, expect the best.

When our worlds crumble, it takes us by surprise.

It was 2018. For some time, my husband and I had been growing apart. Our marriage was suffering and we were at the point of separation discussions. Just as we were making our final decisions and coming to an agreed-upon conclusion, my husband broke his leg. It was traumatic and brought with it added life challenges.

Less than one month later, I broke my wrist. It was a bad break and I needed surgery. During the operation, I experienced heart complications and flatlined on the table. Yes, you read that correctly—I died for a hard twenty seconds. When I woke up, I felt disoriented and foggy, but I had no idea what had happened. After the doctor notified me, I was in shock and had to undergo several post-surgery treatments for my heart in order to ensure that I was fully stabilized.

That feeling of utter astonishment and disbelief has stayed with me ever since. To know that my heart had stopped, that the line on the machine was flat, that I had to be revived, and that it was quite possible I never would have been here writing this today—I am forever changed as a person. As I felt those realities really sink in, I also became acutely aware of how precious life is and how, for some meant-to-be reason, I *am* still here and I am *supposed* to be here. This added gratitude and purpose has made me go harder and stronger in all that I do, most importantly, to be happy and successful. Since that day, I feel a strong desire to take advantage of my second chance in order to forge ahead full force and make a real difference in this world.

You can't wait for the perfect time to be successful.
You can't procrastinate your desires to make a difference.
You can't delay your happiness another second.
Because you never know ...

Since that day in the hospital, my life has been anything but a free ride. Following these two traumatic incidents, my husband and I decided to postpone our divorce. We needed to slow things down and allow ourselves to physically recover. These unexpected health circumstances were God's way of shutting a door. I now realize that when my husband and I originally decided on divorce, while it may have been the right choice eventually, it was not the right time. It would have broken me emotionally because

I was not yet mentally prepared, and I would have suffered far too much. I couldn't see it then, but I do now.

About a year later, we did begin our separation and divorce process. And my, was it ever a process—one which only resulted in a settlement after a year and a half of arduous court visits and negotiations.

Maybe it was a coincidence, maybe it was because I desperately needed a distraction, or maybe it was that I received so much love and support from others during this difficult time, that I felt compelled to give back. Whatever the core motivation, it was in the midst of my messy divorce that I launched my nonprofit initiative, Women in Mining Central America (WIMCA). It's an organization focused on the promotion and empowerment of women in mining, as well as the education of youth around the world on mineral resources and the importance of the mining sector.

It was during this experience that I came face to face with "the noise." By that I'm referring to all the clanging and clattering that surrounds us. Sometimes that noise might be the menial everyday things like advertisements, the dinging notifications on our phones, young children who demand our immediate attention, or flooded email inboxes that tear us away from whatever core activities we're doing. Other times that noise comes in the form of more complicated life situations, as it happened in my case.

In the middle of a divorce and in the thick of what I like to call my passion project, the launch of WIMCA, I found myself the batter at the plate in a game of wicked curve balls. My work visa expired without any chance for renewal because of the global pandemic, making me unable to travel back home to be in the comfort of my family. I was involved in a terrible accident that totalled my car (my son and I were fine, for which I am so grateful, and I believe it was the hand of God that saved us). The same week of my inauguration ceremony for WIMCA involving four continents connected via Zoom, I received a notice from my landlord to vacate our home. One day prior to the inauguration, we hit the pavement and found a property. The evening of the ceremony, the agreement for the property was signed. It was a fresh start and new beginning in every facet of my life.

I knew WIMCA was my newfound inspiration as well as my way to give back and make a difference. I had to do it, no matter what. The noise was all around me. I felt the hiccups and I dodged the curve balls. Today, less than two years later, I am so pleased to say that we have taught children's programs in nine countries, educated and provided training to more than four hundred museum guides in four countries, and helped empower thousands of women in mining through education initiatives in nine countries. It's more than I had planned or hoped for. You see, growth is not always how you envision it—sometimes it is even greater. So, think big. Be conscious of the glass ceiling and don't limit yourself within its perceived confines. It helps to have a support network around you. A sense of community full of nurture and guidance goes a long way, so I encourage you to be mindful of this on your journey.

As entrepreneurs, as women, as mothers, we must trust that special intuition we were given. The noise will always be there, but how much we pay attention to it is up to us. Will we let it distract us? Bombard us? Overtake our vision? Or will we press on and stay on our chosen path despite its inevitable presence? We must train ourselves and stay true to who we are, because we are capable and we are worthy of the success and happiness we strive for.

Since I started working at the age of fourteen, I have been part of a highly underrepresented group: women in mining. I've often been the only woman in the room for years.

Have I noticed that? Yes.

Have I let it intimidate me, hinder my actions, or hold me back? No.

Instead, I have remained on the path that is rightfully mine. I have achieved the seemingly impossible, despite what others think or say. Not only have I done this as a woman, but also as a *Latino* woman.

Most recently, I became a member of the board of directors for a mining company based in the UK. I've been on several boards before, and have even presided some of them, but this is my first paid board position. Once again, I am the only woman at the table, and this time, one of only a handful of women to be on the board of a publicly listed company, one of the few Latinas, and one of the first women in the world under the age of forty to sit on *any* mining board, *ever*.

I now hear a new type of noise. The inner voice noise that has me feeling fearful, insecure, and unsure. But instead of allowing my fears to become my dominant leading force, I've chosen to address and settle that noise from a different angle. Education. I am in the process of taking several courses to equip myself and give myself the confidence for this board position—a position that will enable me to make history. On one hand, I know there will be people watching my every move, making sure I don't falter and that I am living up to their every expectation. On the other, I am aware of all the other women out there who may be looking up to me, gaining confidence and inspiration from my life, and aspiring to do something similar in theirs.

CHAPTER 4: THE COMPASS

It may not be possible to accept a new challenge without fear, but it is possible to accept a new challenge in spite of it.

I have a strong desire to create change in this life. At CTA, I strive to end the stigmas associated with Latin American companies and to prove that we too can provide just as good a service as any other large, enterprise-level North American or European business. Through WIMCA, I seek to redefine and change the narrative of the mining industry in a more positive light. I commit to lifting up and supporting women working in mining in a region that is highly "machista" (male chauvinist) and in an industry that is undoubtedly male dominated. And I pursue a vision to educate youth on the importance of mineral resources and to engage more females in STEM careers.

These are big feats and I know that. The thing is, every goal is a big feat in the beginning. What is yours? What is it that you are driven to accomplish? Does it call for years of academic mastery? Optimum physical aptitude? In-depth knowledge? A lifetime of wisdom?

Whatever your dream requires of you, one thing is for certain: at some point, concrete skill and tangible information will only take you so far, and you'll need to get in tune with your inner compass. When you feel it, listen closely to the direction in which it points you. You'll know when the time is right to tune out the noise, follow your compass, and achieve the feat that, at one point, seemed impossible.

From Me to You:

Your inner compass is real. Don't ignore it—embrace it. Let it guide you to take those leaps of faith that help you grow, achieve, flourish, and thrive in this world.

– Ana

CHAPTER 5:
THE HELM

Do you want to live, and die without anyone knowing you were here?

Be recognized for being you and highlight the mark that you leave on this earth. Think about what makes you unique. Think about what makes you stand out. As we say in business, what is your value proposition?

Mastering the art of standing out is an indispensable skill. Throughout life, whether it's attracting a potential partner, distinguishing yourself at school, competing in sports for that elusive gold medal, or excelling in business where clients must choose you over your competitors, the ability to make yourself shine is a game-changer.

Back when I worked as a television producer, I can vividly recall the daily routine of sifting through a towering stack of press releases sent in by various companies, each hoping for a spot on our TV show. Full transparency, it went something like this: *'Toss, not interested, too similar, just covered this, spelling errors—an immediate 'no,' toss again.'* Then, just like in the fairy-tale Princess and the Pea, I would find the pea, under a ton of media kit folders and press releases, this would be the story that I chose to cover. Why? Because it stood out, captured my attention long enough for me to read and fall in love with the brand.

I've carried this valuable lesson throughout my life, applying it to shape the marketing strategies of numerous businesses. Understanding that standing out in the business world is essential for long-term success, it's your single chance to hook your audience, whoever they may be, and convey, 'You need to choose me, and here's why.'

When establishing my communications firm, I understood that the concept of standing out needed to be an integral part of our mission statement. As we brainstormed ideas for decorating our first office space, we envisioned creating an environment that would serve as a constant reminder of our unique qualities. We wanted every glance from a desk, every stroll around the office, every walk to the coffee machine to reinforce our commitment to being distinct in our industry. We chose a thematic approach based on a series of photos featuring a collection of identical items with one item always standing out as different. My personal favorite was a basket of green apples with a single red apple placed prominently in the center. It was our constant reminder that we needed to zig when the industry zags. These visuals were strategically positioned as the first and last things clients saw during their visits. Leading by example, we wanted our clients to know that we live by our values, to stand out in a positive way, and that we could achieve this for their brand too.

A very valuable lesson I learned occurred during the early stages of launching On Q Communications. With a beginner's, somewhat naive 'you can do anything' attitude, we quickly hit a roadblock when diving deeper into business development and trying to establish a presence in front of potential clients. I've always understood the significance of confidence as the most important outfit one can wear, but at that time, my wardrobe was somewhat lacking.

I was in my twenties, filled with boundless enthusiasm, and had just launched my business, eagerly looking to turn hundreds into millions while aiming to onboard clients. The problem lay in the industry we sought to break into, which was predominantly occupied by seasoned professionals with salt-and-pepper hair, boasting over twenty years of experience, while we had less than five. It was a significant mental hurdle, and negativity began to seep in. Why would anyone choose us, with our limited experience and knowledge compared to our more established competitors?

Looking back now, I would tell my younger self that, despite their extensive experience, our relentless 'go-getter' attitude counted for a hundred times more. Sometimes, a shift in mindset can make all the difference. Our perspective changed during a lunch meeting with one of our mentors, who guided us to see things differently, leading to a path of self-discovery. He made us realize that our youth in that specific industry was, in fact, a tremendous asset that could set us apart. It was our opportunity to be the 'red apple' among a sea of 'green apples' — much like the picture that adorned our office wall.

To explain, this was the very beginning of the social media era and marketing firms were just beginning to embrace it. Facebook had recently taken off, and this terrain was relatively uncharted in the world of marketing, particularly for those who had been in the industry for years. But wait for it... the perfect opportunity lay ahead, with our youth as a significant advantage. We were part of the generation that witnessed the explosive growth of social media, and we saw a chance to make our mark in the business world by harnessing the potential of this digital realm.

This change in mindset led us to become one of the first local firms to incorporate digital marketing as a core service. We successfully demonstrated how social media could generate income for our clients, and our demographic, being 'in the know,' lent us credibility. We were good at what we did, and this new service set us apart from our competitors. From initially fearing competition with experienced industry professionals, we ended up owning this space, with our age becoming a crucial factor that opened the gateway to opportunity.

Standing out is a principle that extends to every facet of business, not solely in sales and marketing. I recall a distinct moment during our hiring process for a junior public relations position when we received numerous résumés, most of which were sent by mail back then, it reminded me of my days in the newsroom sorting through press releases. These résumés typically followed a pattern: recent graduates, some internship experience, seeking a permanent role, exuding confidence and newbie enthusiasm. They were neatly packaged in standard folders, as expected. Then, there was one package that broke the mold and piqued my curiosity. I was eager to open it for one simple reason: it really stood out among the others. It was the proverbial 'pea' in the stack of mattresses.

Inside, I discovered a plastic megaphone attached to a distinctive résumé. This creative approach conveyed that, in a public relations role, one acts as a 'megaphone' for clients, amplifying their messages to the masses. Through this inventive packaging, she demonstrated that she understood what it took to stand out. In an instant, I realized she comprehended our values and the role she would assume. She had taken the initiative to distinguish herself, aligning with our corporate values and the expectations of our clients. We had found our 'red apple' among all the others.

I tend refer to this story frequently, especially when I speak to students and young entrepreneurs. I currently volunteer for an organization that connects novice entrepreneurs with mentors. Through this mentoring role, I'm fortunate to collaborate with driven, budding entrepreneurs who have many compelling business ideas. Together, we navigate the intricacies of their most critical business decisions.

In our initial meetings, I delve deeply into the core question: What sets their company apart? I persistently pose questions until we uncover the golden nugget—their genuine value proposition. Initially, they may stumble in their response, but gradually, a transformation takes place as they gain confidence in their business and the value it promises to deliver.

I've witnessed too many entrepreneurs who overlook the essential task of pinpointing what truly distinguishes their business. I firmly believe that this is the foundational decision upon which everything else hinges. It can be a challenging process, as it often requires a shift in mindset—a shift from conformity to distinctiveness. It's understandable; our world often encourages conformity, from early childhood through school, where we learn to stand in line, wear uniforms, sing in harmony, and avoid speaking out of turn.

While this conformity may suit the school environment, it doesn't serve the business world well. When operating a business, it becomes paramount to showcase your uniqueness and capture people's attention, ultimately persuading them to choose your brand. Needless to say, this act of being chosen holds the key to your future business success.

I serve as an advisor for both a venture capital firm and a university business incubator, engaging in in-depth assessments of companies to determine their eligibility for investment based on their business potential. While this process is intricate and encompasses numerous variables, my primary emphasis lies in the realm of innovation. The true essence of a company's ability to maintain a unique position throughout its growth and consistently deliver value to its target audience is what captures my attention. This unique quality, often referred to as the 'magic' of a business, is what attracts the interest of potential investors and partners.

I've undergone a shift in my approach to evaluating potential ideas and initiating the foundational process of a business. I now find it beneficial to engage in brainstorming sessions for potential exit strategies before advancing. This concept aligns with the core message of this book—when starting a business, it's essential to have a clear sense of where you want your journey to lead. It's about understanding how your business's ultimate destination justifies the path you take, essentially practicing a form of reverse engineering. Questions arise: Is your aim to create a lifestyle business? Or are you envisioning a business you can build with the intent to sell in the future? If the latter, what category of company are you aiming to attract? Could there potentially be a path toward taking your business public someday? It may appear that such forward-thinking is far-fetched at such an early stage, but considering these possibilities can significantly influence your key business decisions.

Knowing your journey will likely bring about various changes, adaptability remains a crucial quality when at the helm. However, the benefit of maintaining a clear vision of your ultimate destination is to provide long-term perspective and direction for the development of your venture. This vision acts as a constant guide, keeping you on course throughout the changing tides of your journey.

Also, remember that it is you at the helm of this journey and deep within you is a clear sense of purpose. Direct your energy towards realizing this purpose. It's the masterpiece waiting to be painted, the story waiting to be written, and the impact waiting to be made. Your journey is one of purpose, meaning, and fulfillment. Embrace it, nurture it, and let it shine brightly, it is your gift to the world.

From Me to You:

You are the artist of your own life. What do you want your masterpiece to look like? What will set it apart and make people want to admire it? Remember that even Picasso thought about this at some point before he put the brush to the canvas. How will you leave your mark on this earth?

– Tanya

A Tale from the Sea

Catherine Tanaka
Fitness, Mindset & Transformation Coach

In this chapter, I will share my story of what it means to be at the helm of your life and how steering your boat is more than always being in control, but rather it means to follow the flow.

My hope is that you see entrepreneurship as an invitation to share your gifts through business and that you can create your own path, paved by what you desire, even if you're not always clear about what you want when you start.

Entrepreneurship for me was a becoming, led by an evolution of self and a desire to have a business that fit into my life, on my terms.

At the time I'm writing this, I am a fitness expert and mindset coach as well as the host and producer of a nationally ranked podcast, *The Body Project Podcast*. I have a successful fitness business where I train clients one-on-one, and run incredible online programs that transform busy women into feeling their best and being their fittest, most energized, and happiest selves.

I believe that fitness is a powerful practice that teaches focus and discipline, completely shifting how people honour who they are and how they live. I am also a mom of two incredible kids, and a wife to a great partner of eleven years. We are a family that loves to experience life, the outdoors, and loves being with people we appreciate.

CHAPTER 5: THE HELM

A Ship Is Easy to Steer in a Calm Ocean

My business is a busy one. I train clients starting at 6:00 a.m. and run coaching programs until 10:00 p.m. some nights. I love my clients and the extraordinary transformations I see them make every day. The truth is that I fell into fitness and didn't realize I could create a thriving business out of it until I was doing it. I want you to see that there are many roads to entrepreneurship, and that aspiring to live a life you love and serving from a place of making a difference is sometimes enough to get you where you want to go. For me, the ocean analogy is so fitting to how I discovered my business path. Prior to the last decade, I feel like I've been at the mercy of a raging ocean without the control of being able to steer my ship well at all.

Looking back, I've lived through a compilation of education and jobs that made no sense at the time. I tried with all my might to control and steer my ship to where I thought it should go, but never felt like I was on the right path. Looking back now, however, I can see that I was guided by the currents of life's ocean, learning how to navigate rough waters to become capable, skilled, and resilient to better navigate and steer my life to *my* perfect blue ocean.

Falling into Fitness

As a half-Japanese kid who was bullied for being Asian and chubby like a rice ball, I very much struggled with finding where I fit in. It wasn't until my high school boyfriend introduced me to weight lifting that things changed. I know this sounds cliché, but fitness changed my life.

As a bullied kid, I never felt proud, supported, or good enough. There was something about lifting weights that was empowering. A deep focus was required to learn and execute movements; I was good at this. There was the practice and discipline of breath and control; my body was capable. With the combination of focus and breath, movement with repetition, the gym became my sanctuary, a place of self-mastery. I call this meditation through motion. Everything about it helped build my confidence. I became strong in my body and in my mind. It changed who I was.

Fragile to fit. Depressed to empowered. Broken to becoming.

In the summer of 1999, I got certified as a personal trainer. Ever since then, I've had a part-time fitness job throughout school, boyfriends, and other jobs. The becoming was a long journey, one that took me many years, more education, and a few other careers before landing back into fitness.

Getting Tossed at Sea

I think it's relevant to share some of where my journey began. A rocky start often gets mistaken for an inability to succeed. I am proof that the start has little relevance to the results. It is through our adaptability and willingness to change course that success can be achieved.

Although I loved working as a trainer, I was set on discovering a "real" career. Being a trainer or just doing fitness was definitely not something my parents approved of. After that summer, I went straight to university, studied kinesiology, minoring in psychology. Kinesiology made sense to who I was at the time. Plus, I was told that to get a career, I needed a degree. Giddy up!

University was hard for me. I did well enough, but learning was effortful and the pressure to succeed was overwhelming at times. I was brought up in a very strict Japanese household with high expectations and I lived with the unspoken pressure of having to be able to pay for school, have good grades, and to be able to do it all.

I now see that these years were my training ground for life. I was getting tossed around at sea between a demanding course load and two jobs; I was just trying to stay afloat. Sometimes staying afloat is just a matter of holding on until you're rescued, or until your skills improve enough to upgrade your boat. So for the three years after university, I took a postgrad diploma to become a dental hygienist. This became the upgrade I needed to thrive in the open waters of life. I had a great career as a registered dental hygienist for over a decade. This is where my ship was in cruise control; I had a stable career with a fitness side hustle.

The Journey into Entrepreneurship

Shifting from the profession of dental hygiene to owning a fitness business didn't happen overnight. The big shift that happened quickly was learning what no longer worked, then *choosing* what I wanted instead. Becoming an entrepreneur was a result of the process of elimination for me. When I took away all the things that didn't work well, I was left with building a fitness business. I was an excellent dental hygienist for over a decade. Dental hygienists are like lawyers or accountants: we are professionals and service providers. I contracted out my dental hygiene services to multiple dental offices, working five to six days a week, fifty-plus hours per week. I was also a great trainer, teaching spin and training at some of the hottest gyms in the city. I loved having it all! Until I didn't.

The Son Has Arrived

I remember while signing my prenup and asking my lawyer, "What happens if I build an empire? Does my husband get half?" He responded that most women, when they have kids, end up changing their career and becoming less ambitious. I thought he was insane and a complete narcissistic jerk. I don't think many entrepreneurial women become less ambitious. I think many become more ambitious and figure out what works best for them, instead of how they can work better for others.

My son Peyton was born in 2012. His arrival was the catalyst to leaving dental hygiene. I wanted to be as present as possible, and it was clear that working crazy hours in hygiene no longer fit into what I wanted. I was adamant to figure it out and make it work. So in all my glory, with only a four-month maternity leave, I made the decision to open up my own fitness studio from home.

This was just the beginning, and it was so much bigger than just me. This was an opportunity for me to *gift* to others how to become their best through fitness, full time. I hustled between being a new mom, cleaning teeth part-time, and recruiting clients to fill my new studio. It was a lot, but it was exhilarating. There was something incredible about serving clients that were mine, not through a gym or leasing space. This was my space, my business, and I facilitated all of it.

My business took off. I started to acquire clients to fill my days and started running group classes daily. Within five months of officially opening, I was pregnant with my daughter Sloan, but that didn't slow me down. I just kept growing my business, working part time as a hygienist, committed to making it all work for me.

Fast forward to today. I have a thriving business that I'm so grateful for. My journey continues to be an evolving path of self-growth and supporting my clients. One of the biggest lessons on my path has come in the last two years. My business got shut down during COVID, and I lost every one of my clients. I witnessed how resiliency is just a word until you have to live it. This is the invitation to take life by the helm and navigate to where you want to go.

Entrepreneurship is inherently about risk. The beauty about risk is that in times of uncertainty, anything is possible. So I had to get resourceful, the Titanic sinking was not an option. Over the last two years, I have created a sustainable business model for my business. This last year was the best year in my fitness business to date. Adaptability is the opportunity of the entrepreneur: create the business and life you want, regardless of what shows up. I am so grateful for all my lessons on this path. My hope is that you can see that there are many roads of possibility for you too.

One of the most powerful exercises I do with my clients is to create a life that they love—a life of being their most vibrant, happiest, content self. I get them to imagine who they want to be in a year, in five or ten years. What does being their most confident, healthy, happy, and best self look like? Who is that person? How do they live? This is the blueprint that leads to the actions of what they need to do and embody now. This will lead them to the person they want to become.

Entrepreneurship is very much like this. What is the business you desire and why, and how can you reverse engineer the strategy to meet that goal? Although my journey didn't work this way, my blue ocean was an evolution of self and a commitment to living my best life.

From Me to You:

Life isn't a dress rehearsal. This is the beautiful journey where we show up for ourselves. We all have unique voyages. May you remember that your willingness to stay at the helm while embracing resilience in raging waters will guide you to your own blue ocean. May you have a thriving business and a life you love. I believe we can have it all.

– Catherine

CHAPTER 6:
THE HIGH SEAS

I call it "my two weeks of doom and gloom." Sound scary? It was.

I was the CEO of a company that I had co-founded 15 years earlier. Recently, I'd bought my business partner's shares, so the company was entirely mine, and I was determined to keep it growing. We had a good group of clients, we were hiring more staff, and the company had always been solid, which seemed like a good sign for our future success. My family life was loving and stable. My body felt strong, I was working out five days a week, eating right, and I felt great. All in all, things were pretty good.

Cue the foreshadow: nothing lasts forever.

Somewhere along the way, I must have crossed the path of a black cat, broken several mirrors, and opened an umbrella indoors because the weeks I had in store for me were going to be a nightmare.

Thanks to my journalling, I can tell you it went something like this:

December 19: *We submitted an offer on a new home, and it was accepted! We had been looking for a house for three years and finally found and bought the perfect location. We decide to do a major renovation before moving in. Our closing date is set for March, which will give us about six weeks before we have to move out of our current home.*

March 8: *Our newly purchased home closes with renovations scheduled to start immediately. There is a lot of information being circulated about a global virus.*

March 9: *We have plans to take the girls skiing, but I woke up not feeling well. I feel like I can't breathe properly. I must have a cold, or maybe the flu? Mark takes them skiing so I can stay home and rest.*

March 10: *House renovations are well underway; the inside of the new house is mostly demolished, there is no going back now! I am home sick with some awful virus and Mark is managing the new house renovation so I can get better. Our eyes are glued to the TV following this new virus, and fear of the unknown is filling our minds. I have an entire house to pack into boxes before moving day, so I feel pressure to get better fast.*

March 11: *A global pandemic is declared. COVID.*

March 13: *I am so much worse. I am weak, lost five pounds, coughing constantly and now wheezing. If I lie flat on my bed, I get the sensation of drowning so I can only sleep if I am propped up on pillows. I really need to see a doctor, but in-person visits are tough to get due to concerns around the virus spreading. Mark leaves to go to our new house very early in the morning and he isn't back until late evening, while he oversees the contractors. Meanwhile, I am busy ordering faucets, paint, fixtures and flooring online because showrooms are empty with everyone working from home. I am not sure if what I am ordering will work in the space, but I have to* *make do with what's available. I am frustrated with the timing of everything.*

March 14: *Mark is moving things along at lightning speed so we can move in as planned. He only comes home to sleep and in another room, to avoid catching what I have. We need one of us to be strong during this time. The kids are home on March break, I am overwhelmed, and now I am worried I might have COVID. Another blow, a call from my client, "We need to pause our work together during these uncertain times." I am sad and frustrated, wondering why this is all happening right now?!*

March 15: *I am lucky to find two walk-in clinics that would see me, but neither will test me for COVID (they are only testing those that have recently travelled). I go to one, but there isn't much they could do to help me. I ask for a steroid for my breathing (that helped me in the past when I had a bad flu) but this medication is in question when it comes to COVID, so they are hesitant. The doctor thankfully prescribes me an antibiotic and a puffer, but sends me off with this: "If you continue feeling short of breath, go to emerg." I am frightened. Cara, youngest daughter, falls ill with the same symptoms. I am not well, but I need to take care of my sick child. Everyone we know is isolating. I have no one to go to for help, out of fear that I would transfer what I have. Mark has to be at the new house; we need it to be ready for our move. I feel very alone and now I'm worried about Cara. I feel like I could cry all day.*

March 16: *As COVID news engulfs our lives, we can't help but wonder if the world as we know it is coming to an end. To make matters worse, Cara has a fever. Then more bad news, another client call, and another client drop-off. The world no longer feels safe, and the calm we once took for granted is now gone.*

March 20: *Our contractors are now hinting that they will be stopping work due to COVID fears. We have to be out of our current house in exactly a month; it is already sold. The new house has no walls, no kitchen, no working washrooms. We will be homeless! While the entire world is avoiding people, we are seeing a handful of new contractors each day at the new house and due to mask shortages, we are using the same and only two masks we have, do they even still work? What will we do if we can't finish our home? We don't feel right staying with grandparents, other family, or friends in fear that we could potentially bring them COVID. Cara is now on two puffers and experiencing shortness of breath. Everything about this is unsettling.*

March 22: *After bottles of medication, throat lozenges, and boxes of tea, I have now lost eight pounds and although I am slightly better, my breathing still doesn't feel normal. I am sure I have COVID. This is the worst virus I have ever had. Then, another client call, another drop-off. Some of our big clients are event based and due to restrictions and closures, all in-person gatherings are on hold. Their businesses are in jeopardy and so is mine!*

This started to be the new trend over the next few weeks, call after call. It took fifteen years to build a business that withered away within weeks.

Within about two weeks, I went from having a flourishing business, a stable household, and a healthy body to losing eighty percent of our client base, the fear of not having a bed to sleep in soon, and a body that could barely carry me.

I felt like waves were crashing into me from every angle. High seas is an understatement for how I felt in the turmoil of it all. It was a fearful time, full of instability, to a magnitude that I've never experienced in such a short period of time. One morning, my daughter Lea walked into my bathroom while I was in the middle of inhaling my puffer — her eyes were full of fear. I realized she was carrying the stress of the household and was worried about everything around her; school was cancelled indefinitely, Daddy was not safe — potentially being exposed to COVID while at the new house — Mommy didn't even have energy to make a meal, her personal items and toys were now inaccessible and packed in boxes. The pressure you feel as a mom to make your kids as comfortable and happy as possible is immeasurable. The look in her eyes was my reality check. I knew that it was time to pull together every bit of strength I had. I realized there was no choice but to keep moving forward, one unsteady step at a time. I felt like if I tried hard, I could see the light. I had faith that if I took care of my body, it would eventually heal. I knew that if we had to live without furniture and a kitchen, while sleeping on blow-up mattresses on plywood in the basement of our new home for a period of time, although miserable, we would get through it and make interesting memories doing so. We had heat, thankfully!

But my business was decimated. All those years of hard work dwindled down to almost nothing. Throughout the entire span of this business, there was never even one year where we weren't profitable, nor did we have a year of uncertainty. Business instability wasn't something that I was familiar with, nor did it consume my thoughts as the CEO. We did everything right: innovation, business training throughout, HR coaches, financial forecasting, proactive business development, convenient office space, happy clients, and work colleagues that felt like family. The devastation was real, with layoffs, loss of wages (mine included), rent that needed to be paid, and all the other implications that come with a failing business, including the dreadful thought of how to go about creating a business development strategy in isolation during a pandemic. Unfortunately, as we all have learned at some point, life happens. You can have your plans but, as the famous singer Drake likes to summarize it: then there is *God's plan*. The pandemic caused so much heartache for so many. I was grieving a major loss. This business was everything to me: my livelihood, my motivation, my history, my career, my happiness. It was an entrepreneurship badge!

Business is a game with a twist. When we are winning, we are successful, but when we are losing, we are not failing, instead, we are learning. I wondered what this lesson was about.

Shortly after, it struck me like a bolt of lightning; this was a game of mindset. With my arms crossed in front, like a protective shield, squinting ahead and moving forward cautiously, I was determined to emerge victorious from this round. Having lost both of my parents at a younger age, it scarred me in a way that is unrepairable. Believe me, I'm well acquainted with the depths of heartache and despair. This surely wasn't going to be the end of me. Instead, this was going to be my chance at a new beginning, a rebirth.

I set new goals for my business and myself as an entrepreneur, and gradually, the turbulent seas began to calm. I made a conscious decision to rebuild the foundation, filling any gaps in the business, harnessing the potential of a new era in communications, reaching for even larger clients, and venturing into the global market.

Fast forward: My business grew and was actually acquired!

Exhale.

This lesson holds true for everyone, not just me; sailing through the stormy seas is a fundamental experience for all entrepreneurs. As Bob Proctor wisely stated, "If you think it, it shall be so." Our mental images shape our reality, and our thoughts guide our actions. Delve deep to uncover your source of positivity, even when negativity surrounds you. Cultivate your mindset and persist in moving forward, even when faced with adversity.

Push harder with focused thinking, and you will find the determination to navigate through rough waters. Your destination is assured. While bruises and bumps are par for the course, you will ultimately conquer the challenges of the high seas.

From Me to You:

The theory of opposites is absolute. It tells us that you can think either positively or negatively, but you can't do both at the same time. Train your brain to choose positive.

– Tanya

A Tale from the Sea

Stephanie Chan
Founder/CEO, myCareBase
Founder/Owner, Home to Home

Practicing law sucks.

I thought this every single day for two years. I was about seven years into my legal career, working as general counsel at a public company and feeling like I had peaked in my current role. While I appreciate that there are plenty of happy lawyers out there, I had suspicions before I graduated law school that it likely wasn't a long-term career for me. After I finished my articling year, I was further convinced of this. However, I had just put myself through law school, and thought I'd better give it a good try. After a short stint at a law firm, I moved in-house at a great company and ended up staying much longer than expected. The work was interesting and I loved what the company was trying to achieve, so I stayed there for eight years.

After working on some great projects and learning lots, the time eventually came when I knew that if I didn't make a career change now, I never would. I felt I had learned as much as I could in my current role. The last couple years before I left the company were unhappy as I dreaded going to work every day and felt like I was suffocating. With each week and month that went by, I could feel my stress increasing to unhealthy levels. I even started getting periodic chest pains. I started musing about what I would do if I quit my job. I could make a lateral move to a different company, but would I eventually come to the same junction? Maybe I could do something completely different, but what would that be, and am I crazy for leaving something so stable and that pays so well?

I coasted in that job for another year before an idea came about that felt it would be worth leaving law for. I finally took the dive in 2007 and left law cold turkey to start my first business in the senior living industry. Then in 2019, I took a deeper dive and started a second business, again related to senior living. What a ride it has been!

When I think back to how I got the courage to dive into entrepreneurship, I don't remember the exact details other than that I was so miserable in my current job that I knew something had to change. I was stagnating and no longer found my career challenging. They say misery attracts more misery, and I didn't want that kind of energy around me. On the positive side, I also remember the incredible support that I received from my close friends who encouraged me and actually helped me come up with the name "Home to Home" and the logo for my first business.

Throughout my journey since I left law, I have talked with others who were scared to leave their careers because they felt they were trained for only one thing. Typically, these people were professionals who had invested a lot of time and money in their education and saw themselves pigeonholed into a specific career. I wish those people could see that they have so much more potential and capability than they realize!

Think of your life as a big journey. If you stayed docked in one place your entire life, it wouldn't be much of a journey, would it? This chapter is meant to inspire and help those who are thinking of taking that jump into entrepreneurship but are scared, don't know what to expect, or just feel there is something holding them back. The rest of this chapter contains some life lessons I've learned that I hope will help others navigate the high seas.

Find Your Purpose

I believe that everyone needs purpose. (Incidentally, I actually believe that everyone needs three things in life: purpose, community, and reward, but more on those other two things later.) Life is sometimes like a jigsaw puzzle. You don't always see the whole picture in the beginning, and many things don't make sense at the time they are happening, but things become clearer when certain pieces come together. Without purpose, you're just wandering through life aimlessly and the pieces of your personal jigsaw puzzle may never come together. It's like going on a sailing trip without a map or chart. Purpose does not have to be a career or tied to money. I have many friends who feel their main purpose in life is to raise a family, and they are great parents. Your purpose also can shift as you go through stages in your life. When I started my first business, I really felt for the first time that I had found my purpose. It was a feeling I can't totally describe, but it felt like there were forces I couldn't see, pushing me down this path.

Prepare for Future Opportunities

When I started my first business, Home to Home, I naively thought that my business degree would give me enough knowledge to prepare for and operate a business. Boy, was I wrong. Just like a long sailing trip, starting a business requires a lot of planning and preparation. In my first few years, I made many mistakes. The support environment for start-ups back in 2007 were nothing like what they are today. There were only a few programs offered in my city that I knew about, and none of them seemed to suit my needs. Nowadays, there is an entire ecosystem dedicated to founders starting a business and the quality of content is amazing. Here are some tips to help you launch a business:

- Do some research and take part in an incubator or accelerator program to learn what it takes to start a business, scale, and raise funding. Despite what you think you already know, I promise you'll learn a lot.

- Join groups that support founders, and network with people who have gone through the entrepreneurial journey. Keep in touch with them because they can help you in the future; and who knows, maybe one day you can help them too.

- Participate in webinars, courses, and conferences where you can improve your knowledge and skills. In addition to the knowledge you'll gain, there may be some speakers and panelists that you may want to keep in touch with. You'll be able to reach out and say that you attended their event as a sort of warm introduction.

- Do some self-reflection about what your weaknesses are and find ways to bolster those skills. One of my areas of weakness is marketing and sales, and that is where I ask for the most help.

- Have a basic understanding of finance. As a business owner, you need to be able to read and understand financial statements, if not at the outset when you start your business, then eventually down the line.

One other thing I would highly recommend is to take some time to really understand the industry in which your business will operate. When I quit law, I took six months to learn everything I could about senior living, and that helped a lot. I contacted others who ran noncompetitive businesses and asked for informational interviews. Many of them were agreeable, and I learned a lot from those meetings. One of the people I met with actually predicted the direction that my business would eventually take, and he turned out to be right!

Expect Rough Waters

The roughest waters are in the first few years, for sure. Getting a business off the ground and generating net positive cash flow might be the hardest thing you'll ever do. Expect that you will experience very high times and very low times. The preparation you will have done and the people that you surround yourself with will be key in helping you through the tough times. Expect that some things will happen that are out of your control, and also expect that there will be times when you won't have any idea what to do. Below are some further tips to help you through these rough waters.

Surround Yourself with Cheerleaders

Entrepreneurship can be rocky at the best of times. It really is like the high seas. One of the best pieces of advice I can give is to surround yourself with people whom I call "cheerleaders," those who believe in you more than you believe in yourself. They do not have to be people who are involved in your business, and actually it is probably better that they're not. They are on the sidelines, to boost your morale when you have tough days, weeks, or months. These cheerleaders are key to your mental health. They can be a friend, mentor, spouse, or family member. Inevitably, at one point or another most entrepreneurs will experience moments of self-doubt, failures of varying degrees, and even times when you wonder if you should just quit. I don't think people talk about the relevance of mental health enough when it comes to entrepreneurship. When I started my first business, Home to Home, it took a very long time to find my first customer. Each day, week, and month that went by without any revenue just increased my depression and self-doubt. Of course, things did get better, but it was a slow process. When I started my second business, myCareBase, I made sure that I had a good support team around me, both inside and outside the business. The best kind of success is achieved with a team, and trying achieve success on your own in many cases may prove impossible.

Expand Your Network and Skills

One of the best pieces of advice I received early on in my career was from one of my bosses who nudged me to volunteer out in the community because it would expand my network and skills in ways that the company I worked at never could. He was so right. After some self-reflection about causes that were meaningful to me, I started volunteering at a charitable organization called Make-A-Wish. Eventually, I joined their board of directors. Although my role has changed over time, my relationship with Make-A-Wish has lasted seventeen years and it has truly been the most worthwhile thing I have done in my life.

Aside from volunteer work, there are lots of ways to expand your network and skills. Look for ways to build your leadership skills outside of your current work environment. Integrate yourself into different communities. I believe everyone needs a community, and some of us may belong to multiple communities. For example, you have the one you live in, your family and friends, your professional network, and perhaps your child's school community. Join an association or club, get involved in a local neighborhood organization, and get out of your comfort zone. You'll meet people that you never would come across in your day-to-day career, and develop skills that will end up complementing your career path. If you do volunteer, I would recommend picking a cause that you truly care about. Being a board or committee member takes a lot of effort, and if you don't have passion for the cause, it is literally just more work. If you feel passion for the cause or it has a meaningful connection to you, it will be much more enjoyable and it won't feel like work at all.

Build Marketing and Partnership Channels

One of the key themes you may notice in this chapter is the importance of surrounding yourself with others who complement and support your goals. No matter what kind of business you have, you'll need to develop marketing and distribution channels to sell your products and services. At this point, partnerships, networks, and collaborations become very important. Think about what those channels might be before your start your business, and develop a marketing strategy as part of a larger business plan. This document will essentially become the map of your entrepreneurial journey. You'll refer to it often and revise it as you shift course throughout your journey.

Embrace Your Vulnerabilities

Once you realize where your weaknesses are, don't be scared to ask for help. After I started my second business, myCareBase, the first year after launch was especially tough. Two things that helped us turn the business in the right direction were expanding our board of directors and forming an additional advisory board. I shifted my mindset to start asking more people for help. I used to worry about not being able to reciprocate, but I realized that if people believe in your mission, they will want to help and in many cases, without asking for anything in return. It takes a small village to accomplish something great.

Leverage Your Strengths

I've lost count of the number of people who have said to me, "You used to be lawyer? What made you embark on something so different?" I would always give the same answer. I took what I'm best at—giving balanced, good advice—and instead of advising companies, I decided to advise people on other things, namely, senior living matters. With my first business, Home to Home, we help seniors and their families with healthcare navigation, transitions, and downsizing, as well as care planning and care management. My second business, myCareBase, helps seniors stay living safely at home for as long as possible by helping them find and manage pre-vetted caregivers and other service providers. With these two businesses, what gives me the most meaning and intrinsic reward is the notion that we are making a meaningful impact on people's lives, at a time when they need the most help. I realized that making an impact is the thing that drives me, and to this day it remains one of the criteria I use to determine how I spend my time and effort.

No matter what career you are in now or what you do next, you will be able to take your own strengths and apply it to the next part of your journey. As you figure out what those strengths are, you will likely discover what drives you, and realize an intrinsic reward in addition to the monetary rewards you receive from your business.

From Me to You:

You are much more capable than you think. In these modern times, there is no reason anyone should feel they are stuck in one particular job or career if they have other ambitions. I want to say to engineers, lawyers, accountants, and anyone else who feels they were trained to do only one thing—you can do anything!

– Stephanie

CHAPTER 7:

THE TELESCOPE

You hold the telescope up to your right eye. You move slowly in a back-and-forth motion, scanning your surroundings. Left and right, left and right. All you see is water. Moving, rippling, it's alive as can be as you and your boat sail together along the surface.

Every hour or so, you pick your telescope back up and search in the distance again. You're comforted only by the grand waters around you until, one time among many, you catch a glimpse of something through the lens. What's that? It's new, it's exciting. Something different has come into view! It just took a little time, patience, and the right tool to see it.

Picture your life as the sea of water around you. Oftentimes, the view is same. Every day you wake up at approximately the same time, you eat the same breakfast, you drive to the same place of work, you exercise the same way, and you spend time with the same family and friends. It's your routine—a sea of sameness. Until your view changes and you discover a new dream to chase after. You steer your boat in a new direction, and just like that, everything looks different.

In my early twenties, my career path really began to take shape and come into full view. Two distinct paths emerged, and I had the strong desire to pursue both — real estate investing and journalism.

Uncovering My Path to Real Estate Investing

I never had any interest in real estate. It was nothing more than the industry my father chose to work in and one I frowned upon because the hours could be so unconventional. I once boldly declared that I would never marry someone involved in the real estate industry. Irony struck, my husband works in real estate. It seems I've become the daughter who fulfilled that very declaration – marrying someone quite similar.

While my father never cared whether or not I made real estate my career, he did care that I had knowledge about this wealth-building asset. He believed it was an integral part of being successful and working toward financial freedom. He even encouraged me to get my real estate licence in my late teens so I could gain a better understanding of the processes involved. Today I view real estate far differently than I did as a young adult. It provides an investment opportunity to build wealth and generate passive income. And almost without even realizing it, it has become a significant part of my professional career.

Many fear it and are overwhelmed by the idea of purchasing property, but I strongly believe it is a pillar of wealth creation that will allow you to pave a path toward financial independence. Many years ago, Mark and I began by buying residential properties close to where we lived. Familiar neighbourhood, familiar home type. We then added value to the properties through strategic improvements that maximized income potential, and then either sold or rented to hold. After we had enough residential properties under our belts, we became more sophisticated buyers and graduated to the commercial side of the market where income generation has more long-term potential. Over the years, together we have focused on a real estate acquisition strategy. It was very intimidating at first. Then again, most things are in the beginning. Now I'm here to tell you that with a spoonful of drive, a cup of education, and a pinch of willingness to take risks, you've got the recipe you need to enter the real estate market and thrive.

Both having entrepreneurial minds, we took what we were doing independently to build our own personal wealth and developed the model into a business that helps others do the same. Through Leacroft Real Estate Management, we help clients acquire property that fits their profile, increase the value of that property, and then add it into our management portfolio that produces true passive income for our clients. For people who lack the time or knowledge to pursue smart real estate investments on their own, the company does it on their behalf, helping them build wealth behind the scenes. The business model was created to be full circle for our clients, from assisting in the acquisition, to performing value-added improvements and repositioning, to managing the portfolio on an ongoing basis. In the end, the client owns great property and receives a monthly cheque as they watch their asset grow in value. Of all the businesses I've been a part of creating to date, this one is most successful in terms of income and growth potential. My mentor once gave me a golden nugget of advice: when you start a business, you need to think about how you can help people make money—and that's exactly what Leacroft Real Estate Management does. Contrary to what most people think, we've shown our clients they don't need to be wealthy to enter the real estate game, they just need to have the will to get involved because there are many creative solutions for entry.

Real estate ownership is so ingrained in my psyche that when I started my first business, I chose not to do the typical and simply lease office space. I wanted to own it. Being savvy with real estate has always been instinctive to me. We purchased the office building through our real estate business, and then my business paid rent to the company. Taking it a step further, the real estate business earned additional rental income by leasing out the extra spaces. Then what we had was a wealth-accumulating asset that was increasing in value and earning extra income in the interim. One more purchase in my game of Monopoly.

Successful business ownership is often about thinking strategically and differently. There are many opportunities; you just need to be willing to see them and take calculated risks when the environment is right. Leverage your position as a business owner, think outside the box, and make intelligent moves that suit your own bottom line.

Uncovering My Path to Journalism

It was going to be anything but easy, but my vision was clear and settling for less was nowhere in my plans. It's extremely difficult to land an on-air broadcast position in journalism. In any city, there are usually only a handful of top journalists with a known presence. I knew how difficult it would be! But my dream was vivid. So vivid, in fact, that I could see it. My passion and dedication were so fierce that I never stopped to question the career path I had chosen. All my focus was on manifesting this dream.

CHAPTER 7: THE TELESCOPE

After graduating from the University of Toronto, I attended a specialized journalism program. I studied hard and tried to learn everything possible about the industry, and I was always willing to go the extra mile. There was a daily ritual I created in order to improve my writing skills: watch the morning news, then try to rewrite the top stories myself and ask my professor to critique them.

Throughout my schooling, there is one day that really sticks out in my memory. I had engaged in an open and candid conversation with one of my professors whom I looked up to tremendously. I'll never forget what he said to me after I spilled my heart out about my aspirations in the world of journalism: "Tanya, there is a one-in-a-million chance for you to land an on-air broadcast position. You should consider having a Plan B."

A plan B?!

I can't lie and tell you that this fleeting statement didn't deflate me, because it did. Not for long, however, because my drive and I quite quickly concluded, "Well, then I have to be that one in a million."

I've spent countless hours rehearsing for my one-in-a-million chance at this. I've talked in front of my mirror for days, announcing and trying to properly pronounce and intonate my voice while speaking to my imaginary national television audience. There wasn't a moment that went by when I wasn't thinking, dreaming, and moving toward my goal. While other students followed the traditional path and waited until their final year of school to secure internship opportunities, I chose a jumpstart. As soon as I entered the program, I met with the director and asked if there was any reason to wait until the final year for an internship. He said no, so I started immediately. I couldn't wait to dive in. I was ready and I was hungry. Everything I knew about journalism up until that point told me this industry was about connections, and the sooner I built them, the better.

My internships spanned numerous roles and I simultaneously focused on my in-class schooling. I left not a single stone unturned. I connected with each and every broadcaster across the city. I didn't care what I was doing, I just wanted to be in a newsroom environment to feel the adrenaline after I heard the words, "And we are on in three, two, one."

Through my hustle, I uncovered an exceptional internship opportunity with a national broadcaster, where I would be given the task to help gather and write the news for the business desk. Woah! This was BIG for me. If I could prove myself in this role, it could lead to more opportunities at the network, and all the while I would be connecting and working alongside reporters and executive producers. The hook? My shift would start at 4:00 a.m.! Did I take it, you ask? Of course I did! There was no option but to walk through every door that opened for me.

During this time, my entire life was turned upside down. When others were eating dinner, I was going to sleep. And when the whole city was sleeping, I was working and watching the sunrise. Throughout the winter, it was especially difficult. I'll always remember those snowy nights (or more accurately, snowy mornings) when I'd wake up to a world blanketed in snow. At 2:30 a.m., I'd find myself out in the cold, shoveling away the snow to ensure I could get my car out on time. Then I'd drive through whiteout conditions across the city to make it to work on time. The thought, "what am I doing?" entered my self-talk frequently. When it did, I always remembered the voice of my parents: "If you want something bad enough and work hard toward your goal, you will eventually reach it." The thought of "reaching it" was just too sweet to let anything

CHAPTER 7: THE TELESCOPE

get in my way. This internship was a great learning experience, both personally and professionally.

Through my internships, I was determined to understand the inner workings of a newsroom. I carefully observed professional journalists at work and took every learning opportunity presented. Each morning around ten o'clock, the reporters would get assigned their story and I would often shadow them for the day. I would learn how they chased the story and packaged it. I would ride with the reporter and camera person to do on-location interviews. Breaking news was always so exciting! They would teach me how to ask the right questions, and I would watch them write and then tape their on-camera closing. We would take the content back to the station and I would sit in the editing room with the reporter, observing how they pieced it all together in time for the six o'clock news. It was incredible to be a part of it all, and this was the best form of learning I could have ever asked for.

When we have clear goals, it's essential that we make them known. You never know to whom you're talking or what ambitious conversations might lead to. I choose to think that the universe is always conspiring to make you a success. And that's why I stopped at nothing to propel forward toward my end goal, and also why I had no qualms about stating my objectives to the well-known reporter I found myself shadowing one day at Queen's Park (government building). Sure enough, the universe heard me, and that connection led me to land my first real job in the industry as a junior producer. For several months, I worked diligently to prove myself in this position, all the while making it clear to my superiors that my end goal was to be hosting my own show. At this point, I was shooting for the stars!

Then the incredible happened. In just six short months, my dream of hosting a show came true. The production company was launching new a health and beauty show that was to air nationally every Sunday and I was offered the position to be a producer and the host. I had made it! It's the moment when all my efforts and aspirations came to fruition.

The first time the show aired was a big event. My entire family gathered in our living room, where we watched. It was one of the proudest moments of my life. Everything about it was thrilling and I relished it all. What an experience it was to be a TV host! Fashionable clothes were sent to me to wear on the show, I worked with a stylist and every month I had a new hair style or colour, sometimes I would get stopped by people in public who complimented me on the show!

It really was a dream come true. I was on my way. Nothing was going to hold me back. CNN, CBS, ABC News—all the big names were on my radar for the future.

Sometimes, seeing nothing but a sea of sameness when you gaze through your telescope is beneficial because the moment you recognize something different you notice it immediately and appreciate it against the uniform waters.

Pick up your telescope often and look through it with excitement each time, knowing that in any given moment, you might uncover something distinct and amazing.

From Me to You:

You will never bring down someone who is committed because someone who is committed is already up.

– **Tanya**

A Tale from the Sea

Sandra Gabriel
President, PR & Communications, 360 Marketing & PR

tel·e·scope
noun
An optical instrument designed to make distant objects appear nearer, containing an arrangement of lenses, or of curved mirrors and lenses, by which rays of light are collected and focused and the resulting image magnified.

Distant objects appearing nearer

It's safe to say that I had a vision for my life before I even knew what an "imaginative" vision was.

Growing up, my aunt Minevra was the only person I knew working in the business world. At first, I didn't know exactly what she did, but I knew she worked in a downtown office in Montreal, and I always admired and appreciated that she was a woman in business. Many women who immigrate from other countries go into health care and personal support work, but my aunt had taken a different path and became an accountant. Knowing about her work broadened my vision and gave me permission to be unique.

I've been told that we are the product of the five or six people we spend the most time with, and in a lot of ways, that is true. However, in my case, as the vision for my life began to set in and take a different path, that myth was quickly dispelled. Not many people around me aspired to business and entrepreneurship, yet I was so drawn to it that it eventually became my reality.

From the time I entered college, business and entrepreneurship have been my career focus. At the time, I didn't know what kind of business I wanted to pursue; I only knew that business was going to be the path for me. Suddenly, I was researching what it takes to start and run a business and what resources are available to start-up businesses. I became so wrapped up and excited that I was quickly navigating into the life I was going to live. I investigated everything from registering a business to marketing a business to managing finances. The more intrigued I became, the more I continued to dig and see myself as an entrepreneur and business owner.

When I moved to Toronto from Montreal in my early twenties, it wasn't to party or find love, although those were bittersweet benefits. I continued my education, sought well-paying corporate jobs, and pursued entrepreneurship, all because I had a vision. Imagining a life of being my own boss and helping other businesses was an experience in the horizon of my mind that came near, and boy did I ever reach for it.

The definition above talks about an optical instrument, and for the purpose of this part of the chapter, the optical instrument is your eyes. Since your eyes feed the mind and soul, what you do with that information creates your mindset and fuels your passion. If you see a particular lifestyle you want to live or the type of work you want to do, then you have to decide to pursue your dreams and not let fear hold you back. I know you will find that as you take steps toward the life you want to live, what was once a distant object will begin to appear nearer.

CHAPTER 7: THE TELESCOPE

Curved Mirrors and Lenses

As I got older and began to get a grasp of what it meant to shape my future, I realized that the vision I had for my life was very different than the vision that my parents had for me. The lens through which I saw my life put me on a journey to differentiate myself, especially where family is concerned—not many people in my immediate family went to college or university or decided to start their own business, which is the case for a lot of entrepreneurs, especially women and moms/wives. I have at least one cousin who chose the road of becoming a stay-at-home mom and wife while her husband worked. It put a huge pause on her entrepreneurial pursuits. The decision to branch out and do a new thing definitely requires that you hold to that vision, but it is often very difficult to do.

When money got tight, I had people telling me to get a job, and it was the last thing I wanted to hear. In their minds, they were being supportive, so I can't fault them for that. What they didn't know was that it was like a punch to the gut every time I heard it. Getting a job meant less time for my business, which would likely mean giving it up altogether, and I was not prepared to do that in any way, shape, or form. The vision had taken hold of me and would not let go.

Like with a telescope, the arrangement of curved mirrors and lenses represents the distorted perspectives and images of you by others, and those perspectives are part truth and part lie. You will most definitely have people in your life who believe in and encourage you, but there will of course be those who are not as supportive; what's worse is that those less supportive people are often friends and family. The people who know and love you the most can sometimes be the least supportive, and that's where you find yourself going against the current.

It can be difficult to build something like a business on your own. Those days when you could really use support, the people you would lean on are only applying more pressure and reminding you that you don't have money, you're getting older, and a job can feed your pension and protect your retirement plans. I don't know about you, but retirement is not something that keeps me up at night. As an entrepreneur, I see myself doing what I love until my last day on earth.

If you believe the negative or positive things that people say and do to you, then it will have a negative or positive effect on you and what you believe about yourself. This is what makes it important to continue to press on because the more you walk toward that vision and see results, your confidence builds, and your confidence begins to draw elements of that vision toward you. Suddenly, you're making connections and winning opportunities that confirm you're on the right track.

Collected and Focused

It wasn't until I had been in business for seven or eight years that I really began to believe in what I was doing. I had more clients coming in and that helped build my confidence. All my business was coming through referrals (it still is), which is a huge testament to the work I'm doing.

In all of this, I kept researching trends in the world of business and entrepreneurship. I went back to school and studied to receive my public relations certificate and a bachelor's in communications, along with a few courses in marketing and project management training. At this point, I felt so accomplished and really good about myself. I had learned so much and honed my craft beyond what similar businesses had been doing, and I felt

CHAPTER 7: THE TELESCOPE

so official that it brought me to another level of hope, which really sharpened my focus.

I can't say that things started turning around for my business right away, but I had certainly levelled up, as I now had the educational credentials to back me up as a professional in my field, but it would still be a while before I progressed to the next level in business.

As a matter of fact, I fell on hard times and I had to move back home to Montreal after I had been living in Toronto for eleven years. In my mind, being back home was the perfect opportunity to focus on my business without having to worry about the rent. I stayed in Montreal for five years before I finally gave in and decided not only to move back to Toronto and try again, but to also get a job so I could rebuild my life. At the time, I was going through all kinds of tests and MRIs and CT scans and ultrasounds because I had found a suspicious lump in my breast. Just as I was planning to restart my life, I was diagnosed with stage 4 metastatic breast cancer — a terminal illness. Talk about a plot twist!

This is the point where one might quit and spend their remaining years focusing on their health, but the vision for my entrepreneurial life had me locked and focused. In my mind, this was the time to dig in my heels. With a diagnosis like mine, my oncologist didn't bother to give me chemo or surgery. My treatment was so light that I'm not in pain or suffering in any way, aside from some hot flashes because my ovaries were shut down to keep estrogen away from my estrogen-feeding cancer cells. To be honest, my life has never been better. My diagnosis gave me permission to live more boldly and confidently than I ever have, and the aspirations for my business only grew stronger.

Rays of light, which are collected and bring focus to the telescope, are equivalent to your hopes and dreams that shine through and help keep you going. When you've spent enough time building confidence, you begin to see amazing things happening in your life. Suddenly, all hands are on deck and it's smooth sailing; you have clients, a team, experience, and profits. However, that vision is still in the distance. The beauty about getting to this part of the journey is that you are so focused that it would literally take a tsunami to knock you down, and even then, you can keep going. The good news is that storms don't last forever.

The Resulting Image Magnified

Fast forward to 2020. We're about to embark on a global pandemic, and the floodgates decide to open on my business. With the order to work from home, I'm finally able to get my long-awaited internship program going for PR and communications students. Having the extra help meant I could take on more business and higher-profile clients, which increased revenues. It didn't hurt to receive a COVID relief grant either, which meant I could pay even more people to join the team. By 2020, I had been in business for fifteen years and I finally began to see the true fruits of my labour. The image or vision had magnified, and I was living in it.

It truly does pay to keep going when you feel all hope is lost. Sometimes, moving past the storms and setbacks reveals things to us about ourselves, which is just what we need to see us through life's obstacles.

When it comes to my vision, there's a scripture that I live by that says: "For the vision is yet for an appointed time; But at the end it will speak, and it will not lie. Though it tarries, wait for it; Because it will surely come, It will not tarry" (Habakkuk 2:3, NKJV).

In other words, your vision exists even though you may not see it right away; it's definitely there. Having patience helped me stay the course, and it's often what gets people to the point of breakthrough. However, if we choose to give up because of the naysayers or difficult circumstances, then the vision becomes a dream deferred.

My advice is this: Keep working, keep moving forward, and keep fighting for what is yours. Endure the tears and the frustration. Celebrate every win, big or small. Keep in mind that all the energy you pour into something will never go to waste if you don't give up. Even though it seems to take forever, wait for it because it will surely come. When you get to the point of realizing your vision and living it out, the feeling can only be described in the words of Johnny Nash who says:

"I can see clearly now the rain is gone. I can see all obstacles in my way. Gone are the dark clouds that had me blind. It's gonna be a bright, bright sun-shiny day.

– Johnny Nash, "I Can See Clearly Now"

From Me to You:

It is in the pursuit of our vision that we are shaped, moulded, and becoming. It's a wonderful journey as long as you don't let the waves and storms scare you away.

– Sandra

CHAPTER 8:
THE CREW

Who is your crew?

Mine includes my husband, two daughters, best friends, brothers, sisters, several close friends and colleagues. A small group of special people in my life.

I assume this is similar to what most people would say. But let's question this assumption.

How do you complete big projects? *It's thanks to your crew!*
Who picks up your kids to enable you to finish working after 3:00 p.m.? *Your crew!*
Who handles your invoicing or accounting? *Your crew!*
Who assists in keeping your home clean and organized, allowing you to concentrate on work and family? *Your crew!*
Who prepares your Starbucks latte so that you can stay alert for in meetings? *Your crew!*
Who supports you if your internet goes down at work? *Your crew!*
Who provides you with business advice when you seek it? *Your crew!*
Who assists you in securing financing when it's needed? *Your crew!*
Who helps you in staying grounded during challenging times in life? *Your crew!*

CHAPTER 8: THE CREW

You get the picture.

When you consider the number of people in your life who support you every single day, it's quite remarkable. They surround you, providing unwavering support, and enabling you to achieve daily success. Without them, well I believe you know the answer. For entrepreneurs, those who help carry the load in your life become even more indispensable. Building something of value on your own is not just challenging; it's often impossible. And even if you somehow reach the pinnacle, what's the fun if you can't share the joy?

My recent solo business travels highlighted a certain element that's lacking for me during these trips. It's not a shortage of excitement or a love for travel. Instead, it's because every time I immerse myself in a new city, meet a client, have a fantastic initial encounter, secure new business, or have a negative experience, my immediate urge is to share these experiences. I often catch myself wanting to look to my right and left, only to realize there's no one there to share in the moment. This realization has emphasized the significance of having a crew, as it not only amplifies moments of success but also lightens the burden during tough times. My crew is my lifeline, my support system, and, most importantly, a source for joy.

Your crew helps you to be the best version of yourself.

The true worth of my crew became apparent when I was blessed with my first pregnancy. At that time, my business was in growth mode. I was working tirelessly, committed to witnessing my business reach its full potential. Motivation was at an all-time high, soaring at 110 percent. I was deeply involved in initiatives to support the growth of women-owned businesses, fully immersed in the realm of female entrepreneurship, and enjoying every moment. I had a consistent belief in entrepreneurship as the ultimate path, and my commitment was unshakable. I was juggling it all: maintaining a healthy lifestyle, adhering to a consistent workout regimen, nurturing my business, and still managing to spend quality time with friends (with no concept of curfew). I was riding the wave of feminist empowerment, with the belief that women could conquer all.

One day, I woke up, peed on a stick, and it changed everything.

Within a few weeks, my priorities changed drastically. My mind went from all business all the time, to being focused on the health and wellness of the baby growing inside me. My friends faded into the background. My chip cravings overpowered my desire to eat salad. My rigorous exercise routine became a thing of the past, and my body felt exhausted around the clock. I was forced to acquaint myself with the concept of napping. I suppose my previous fervor for feminism seemed to have lost its luster.

My initial intent was to take a very brief leave, after all, I had a business to run! I underestimated one thing: the baby-mama bond.

On February 24, 2009, at 5:16 a.m., I had the privilege of meeting my daughter Lea for the first time. A girl! I had always envisioned being a mother to a girl—complete with pink bows, tutus, and all the joys that come with it. It was the greatest joy and everything else in my life took a backseat. The whirlwind that usually accompanies bringing a newborn home is a blur, but one moment stands out from the haze of those early days. The first time I found myself truly alone with Lea. Mark had just returned to work, and it was just her and I, ready to take on the world together. Instead of following the usual routines of taking her for a stroll, feeding her, or letting her nap, I simply cradled her in my arms with gratefulness. I gazed at her and started talking. In that moment, she was my diary. I shared with her the experience of pregnancy, the profound moment of childbirth, and my ongoing journey into motherhood. I expressed my dreams for her to have a life overflowing with happiness, health, and an insatiable hunger for knowledge. I encouraged her to always be compassionate and kind, fostering love and respect for others. I promised to support her as she follows her ambitions in her chosen path. I told her that I want her to be brave and resilient, unafraid of life's challenges, and to live a life without limits. Most of all, I wish for her to discover her unique talents and gift them to the world in her own unique way. She looked back at me, her eyes filled with wonder. It marked our first profound bonding experience, one etched in my heart forever. At that unscripted moment, as I was talking, I realized the paramount importance I placed on the people in my life who support me, whom I rely on, and whom I hold dear — my crew. I told her that as she embarks on her life journey, I wish for her to find the wind for her sails from those that support and love her, enabling her to reach her greatest dreams.

Motherhood introduced me to an array of new challenges I had never even fathomed. It was an entirely new universe for me. As an entrepreneur, I have the tendency to look at the world through a business lens. I approached motherhood like a CEO: managing operations to navigate each day, serving as the human resource department when seeking a babysitter, applying marketing principles when selecting baby products, and adopting a financial perspective when tracking feedings and diaper changes. After a few weeks, I began to find my rhythm. It astonished me how demanding and rapid the learning curve was. In the quiet moments of the night, as I was feeding Lea, I often thought about how much I had grasped in such a short span. A growing sense of pride grew within me, reminiscent of the feeling I experienced when nurturing my first business. I was running a tight ship and I really started to enjoy my new mom life. Around that time, I received a call from a friend who was checking in on Lea and she casually asked, "When are you thinking of going back to the office?" Work?! I couldn't think of anything but trying to get enough sleep. And just the thought of leaving Lea to go into the office for the day was too much for me to handle.

My mind started racing. How was I going to manage being a present mom for Lea and run my demanding business at the same time?

Here is something you might not expect: What if I told you I took eighteen months off for maternity leave to enjoy my baby and came back to a flourishing business? Well, it's true, and it was thanks to my crew.

When I decided to start this business venture, I knew the importance I placed on work-life balance and I knew that I wanted to cherish all that it was to be a woman, including having children. I co-founded the business with someone that held similar values. We decided to leverage our womanhood and planned to take turns having babies so that our business would never skip a beat. Realizing how rare this is, it actually worked for us. Five kids later and seventy-two months of maternity leave (she had a set of twins) and we did it! I understand there are many solutions for how a woman in business can handle leave, but at the time, just like how you sometimes feel no one can take care of things quite like you can, I felt the same with my business and baby. My business partner was the best "business mom" I could have hoped for. I was back cheering on feminism once again! She supported me and I supported her in our personal decisions and with our business. Without each other's support, we may have lost special time with our little ones, or our business may have slowed down. Never was I happier that I made the decision to start a business with a partner. It gave me freedom and stability at the same time.

Having two daughters makes me really think about what it means to be a woman and I find it so important to raise them to be confident, lead successful business lives, but still live the joys that come with our gender. The fact that they are females should never hinder them. I want them to see and experience all the beautiful delights that life will bring them, but I never want it to be a lonely journey, nor does it have to be. I find myself coaching my girls to seek out people that lift them up, whether it be friends, family, or mentors. Every woman needs her crew. Life isn't always sunny. Your crew will always be there, through the sun *and* clouds.

The people that surround us and support us are the real champions, the ones who pick us up when we can't stand up on our own. Those who we lean into when we have nothing left inside of us. It's the cheerleaders in your life that push you to cross the finish line and the people that give love when we don't even know we need it.

As you build your vision, identify your crew, lean on them, learn from them, enjoy their presence in your life, and always show gratitude.

From Me to You:

A ship without a crew will never leave the dock.

– Tanya

A Tale from the Sea

Lexi Miles Corrin
Founder & CEO, WAXON Laser + Waxbar

It was made of wood I had collected from the forested area surrounding our family cottage. In the centre were two oak tables, which I decorated with pinecones and greenery. Amidst the décor were bowls of assorted chocolate bars and a variety of canned pops. This was my snack bar.

I was ten. And I was an entrepreneur.

Okay, okay. I know it wasn't making news headlines, the chocolate bars melted and the pop was warm, but it was entrepreneurial nonetheless! Looking back, it's clear to me that I possessed the entrepreneurial mindset from a very young age. My father was an entrepreneur, and I always admired the work life he built around that. I didn't want to *have* a boss, I wanted to *be* one.

Fast-forward to my early twenties. I landed a career in operations-based consulting where it was my job to consult businesses in a wide range of industries with one key goal: drive results. It was here where I learned how companies operate, the ways in which they make money, and different methods to drive process efficiencies. It was a grueling, high-pressure role that had me travelling constantly and working long hours. I eventually left and consulted on my own for a while, until about the age of twenty-five, which was when the WAXON business idea made its way into my mind.

The concept was born out of two personal experiences: 1) my visit to a quick, easy, and painless wax-only spa in Arizona, and 2) the lack of "good" waxing solutions in Canada! When I say

CHAPTER 8: THE CREW

"good," I mean not paying an exorbitant price for a nice wax, not being forced to give up half your day, and certainly not hiding behind a grimy shower curtain at a spa that offers a million other services. There had to be a better way.

Immediately, I began to put all my consulting experience to work on my idea. I Googled, dove into the competition, researched far and wide, and put together projections for the potential business. The numbers added up and I started to plan for the opening of the first WAXON location in Toronto's Summerhill neighbourhood. It was during this planning process when I proved what I could do best: operations. But it was also a pivotal moment in my career when I realized that I couldn't do everything. No one can reach their destination alone, and what fun would that be, anyway?

I was *not* an esthetician.

And that was one of the most important components of the business.

In order for WAXON to have any chance of success, I needed to hire the perfect crew to accompany me through the unchartered waters ahead.

The role of manager (with esthetic experience) was the very first to be filled. Hyperaware of the fact that esthetics has a history of breeding catty work environments, I was committed to changing the industry's poor reputation. I took my time, conducted thorough research, and followed a very meticulous process behind the scenes in order to ensure that the manager I hired for WAXON's first location was perfect.

The first person you hire in your business sets the tone of your entire culture.

This woman certainly set the tone. While she started at WAXON as a manager a decade ago, she has been my vice president of operations for the last four years. She is my right-hand colleague, living and breathing the brand values that mean so much to me.

I'm a "think big" kind of person and my initial growth plan for WAXON was one hundred locations within five years. WAXON has been in operation just over ten years now, and (drumroll please!) we have twenty locations across Canada. Having said that, we currently have an aggressive growth plan in place to open an additional ten locations by the end of 2024.

If I look at only the numbers, I can't help but feel the twinge of disappointment that comes along with falling short of your own expectations. But it only lasts half a second before I am overwhelmed with pride for how far we've come as a corporate team, business, and community. We have brand cohesion, culture adoption, and business strength from the ground up. Where others might have opened additional locations in lieu of building internal relationships, I did the opposite. I focused on my team because I'm a strong believer that your business is only as good as the people behind it. If I had chased the numbers and rushed WAXON's growth in the beginning, I wouldn't have the level of culture or quality of service that have become synonymous with our name today. The way I see it, these people have invested their time and skill in WAXON and my vision behind it—which, by the way, was nothing more than a hunch at the start. I take this to heart, and I will do whatever I need to do to ensure their long-term career success.

As I continue to maintain and construct the team around me, I surround myself with experts to fill in my gaps and do what I cannot: esthetics, waxbar management, marketing, public relations, and finance—yes, definitely finance. I foster relationships grounded in mutual respect and collaboration. The business is one that welcomes mistakes and praises vulnerabilities. We all make mistakes, and WAXON celebrates those as stepping stones, not failures. Instead of passing judgments, we take ownership, listen to one another, discuss what we've learned, and talk about solutions moving forward.

People are innately nervous about failure. I consider it my job to reframe that.

In our executive monthly meetings, we talk openly, candidly, and productively. I explain that there is no shame at WAXON. It's a safe space where we can feel confident in our own skin. I always go first and share my wins, but also my mistakes over the last thirty days (which I remind everyone are inevitably bigger than any mistake they'll ever make), reflect on what those mistakes have taught me, and state my plans for the future month. It's a humbling and vulnerable moment, the process of which has made each and every one of us stronger as a result.

You can never focus too much on your crew. It's impossible. Because if you take the time to nurture and grow a magnificent one, there's no telling all the ways it will support you. The people in your crew are the ones who are at your side through sun and rain, through still air and howling winds, through calm waters and crashing waves. They're committed even when there's no shore in sight.

Eight years into my business, I knew the strength of my crew. But it wasn't until the COVID-19 pandemic began crumbling everything in its path that I truly understood the depth of its value. Company-wide, WAXON employs 150 women. One hundred and fifty *incredible* women. When COVID first touched down in Canada in March of 2020, we were forced to close all of our locations. Just three days prior, my second child, Clark, was born, and needless to say, emotions (and hormones) were running wild. Before I knew it, without a choice and tears streaming down my face, I was in the midst of temporary layoffs.

To my incredible surprise, while I felt the need to be there for *them*, my employees were there for *me*. They continually reached out, provided their support, and reassured me they weren't going anywhere. Together, we rallied and worked hard to keep our crew engaged through regular Zoom meetings, virtual cocktail hours, weekly meditation and coaching sessions, email newsletters and keep-in-touch initiatives. Members of my management team worked without pay for far too long, and said they'd do anything to see WAXON survive. We maintained 95 percent of our staff regardless of the fact that from March 2020 to July 2021, WAXON was closed for a total of 322 days.

During the latest and longest lockdown of seven months, I kept my executive and management teams in their full-time positions and took on debt. I did this in an effort to advance the business for our next phase. Without the day-to-day operations of fourteen locations to concern ourselves with, we were in a position to meet, plan, dig deep, and set up WAXON for success moving forward. This resulted in an aggressive growth plan that we are so excited to see come to fruition.

I couldn't have done this alone in a million years. WAXON would be bankrupt and long gone had it not been for my crew. And that is something I will never forget. The solidarity of these women and of the team we are together drives me now more than ever before. I am determined to continually grow WAXON, crush the stigmas associated with esthetic work environments, build and nurture the crew, help every member on my boat to realize personal success, and to follow my passions through

CHAPTER 8: THE CREW

every season. My newest feat will be opening ten locations (while having twins!). Because I can. Because of my crew.

Remember, your crew isn't only that which applies to your business, but also your life. My husband is in the franchise business too, and thank goodness because he guided and supported me through an extremely difficult process in 2020 and 2021. On the personal side, who are those individuals who lift you up? Who support your every move? Who believe in you and your vision? Who love you for everything that you are?

A strong support team is critical to your overall success. Focus on those who believe in you and your journey.

For me, this means surrounding myself with likeminded people, both in my personal life and my business life.

While COVID represents my toughest business challenge yet, it's not the only time I struggled professionally.

Entrepreneurship can be lonely at times. Particularly when I was younger and single, I felt overwhelmed and utterly alone in my business. I got pulled in bad directions, and with no crew to prevent me from drowning, WAXON almost sailed out to sea without me on it. There were financial strains the likes of which had the CRA calling me for money, and poor decisions to bring misaligned investors onboard at a time of desperation (who, thankfully, were let go shortly after).

But I always knew this business was meant to thrive. Through thick and thin, years ago and most recently during COVID's challenging times, I've had the careers and livelihoods of so many women resting on my shoulders. And that is something I don't take lightly. So, I never give up.

This is a long-term game we're playing as entrepreneurs. We need to stay focused and hone in on what really matters to stick around. For me, that continually takes me back to my crew, the relationships I have with all of its members, and the work environment I foster as a result.

At WAXON, I develop and maintain the culture I am so proud of in a few ways.

1. **Lead by example.**

    I practice what I preach and I stay true to what I say. People expect out of me what I expect out of them. The last thing I'm interested in is "yes people" because I am well aware of the fact that I have good ideas and terrible ideas, so I need people around me who aren't afraid to tell me both.

2. **Know the importance of every hire.**

    One bad wave can demolish your boat. If there is a hiring issue at WAXON, I rectify it immediately to preserve our culture.

3. **Respect.**

    I show, teach, and encourage respect. It sounds simple, but it is genuinely a lot of work to show people true respect.

4. **Results and measurements.**

    The business and the crew are equipped with guardrails and goal posts. This way, everyone knows their expectations and responsibilities, and we are all on a ride of continual learning and growing. Being humble and

5. **Be real.**

    I foster an environment that revolves around *being real*. That means having candid conversations to clear the air as quickly as possible, keeping an open-door policy, maintaining honesty, welcoming mistakes we can learn from, and celebrating and empowering women!

agile are not qualities, but rather requirements on the WAXON team.

These actions that I live and breathe as a leader are reflected in WAXON's core values. And it is these values that shape our culture, fuel our crew, and keep us being generally awesome in our industry.

It's not easy, but one thing I can say for certain is that we all love what we do. We're passionate women who take dreams out of our heads and bring them into our daily realities. We have vision and purpose in what we do. Coming to work is something we look forward to, not dread. I've gone so far as to confront certain individuals over the years and have actually encouraged them to go find their passion because it had become clear that their role at WAXON was no longer it.

When you do what you love, your work is exceptional, and when you don't love what you do, it shows. You shouldn't be there. No hard feelings, no problems. We all deserve to find what we're passionate about so we can bring it to fruition. When we find it, we must breathe life into it. To make it something real.

It will come at a price, however. Because achieving true work-life balance is bullshit. You'll need to make choices. You'll have to determine what matters most to you at any given point in time. You'll find what works and you'll ride the waves, but it is a juggling act—one that can, and likely will, result in dropped balls. That's part of the journey, so embrace it and carry on.

As you venture out to sea, keep your eyes open and your heart full. Figure out what it is that makes you want to set sail every day. And once you do, be ready for full mast no matter what the weather forecast may be. Trust your instincts, go with your gut, and know in your soul you can succeed. Then build the perfect crew around that vision to help you get there.

From Me to You:

You don't need to go it alone.
And you shouldn't.
Instead, focus on building, nurturing,
and caring for your crew.
Then watch how far your boat sails toward the horizon.

– Lexi

CHAPTER 9:
THE PERFECT STORM

As the saying goes, without rain, there would never be rainbows. I weathered a storm, and it ultimately revealed my own vibrant rainbow.

I had turned a corner, navigating the tumultuous waves of the pandemic and its impact on my business. It was time for a new stage in my business and my life. My communications firm had finally started to pick up speed; we were welcoming new clients, and former clients were slowly returning. On the surface, everything appeared settled – we had finally moved into our new home, my daughters had smoothly transitioned to a new school, and my husband's business was also growing exiting the pandemic. All the pieces were in place for a brighter future, except for one thing, I wasn't seeing brightness. The spark that usually ignites me was dim, but why? After a self-reflection session (a habit I've cultivated) I recognized that a part of me felt unfulfilled. I found myself attracted to new ideas, other industries, I would scroll through my social feeds finding myself researching businesses, exploring venture capital groups and even googling start-ups. Something significant was unfolding within me; I was yearning for change.

I had spent two decades in the field of communications, and while the industry had already undergone significant transformation with the advent of social media, the most profound shift I witnessed occurred during the pandemic. It was as if I had gone to sleep in one world and awakened in another. In this new landscape, TikTok personalities had risen to the status of celebrities, social media dominated the headlines of marketing trade magazines, and brands found success by leveraging micro-influencers to build awareness. The media industry had redefined "pay to play," making it very difficult for brands to secure media coverage without substantial budgets.

With experience on both sides of the media, I came to realize that traditional journalism had evolved. The pursuit of compelling stories was often influenced by financial constraints. While I acknowledged that this was the direction the industry was headed, I grappled with the inherent bias it introduced. Alongside this, the monotony of selling the same type of business, the routine nature of client pitches, almost templated RFPs, and the prospect of competing in an ever-changing market, especially against Gen Z, no longer fueled my motivation in the same way.

It became evident that, despite the success of the business, I was no longer passionately engaged as I once had been. I recalled the wisdom of Kenny Rogers: "If you're gonna play the game, you gotta learn to play it right. You've got to know when to hold 'em and know when to fold 'em."

I want to play the game right. It was time for my next chapter.

I could sense rumblings from within. What had long remained dormant was now rekindling. The sensation was not unfamiliar; I had experienced it several times before and recognized it almost instantly. It was my entrepreneurial spirit knocking. I was ready to

CHAPTER 9: THE PERFECT STORM

embark on a new journey and build a business around it, all while immersing myself in the passion it brought. There was something I was in pursuit of, a fresh path that was gradually revealing itself.

I opted for a proactive approach that didn't involve waiting for things to happen. Instead, I took active steps to tap into my networks. I reconnected with former colleagues, engaged in conversations with my mentors, attended events, and joined new clubs and networks. I also spent a lot of time just thinking (a *lot*). It was as if I were engaged in a mental game of chess, constantly experimenting with different moves on the board of possibilities. I would make a move, assess how it felt, and determine whether it was wise or not. My mission was clear: I was determined to uncover my next strategic move.

What you put into the world is what you will get back. I know that the law of attraction would work in my favour, even if it took some time. It was months and months of the same, but I had patience and trusted in these principles. I realized that this was something I needed to work through alone, and being that my ideas were too still too fragile to withstand external critique, I chose to keep my thoughts to myself. I realized it was an internal journey with a known destination; now it was about figuring out how to get there.

As I drifted to sleep after an exhaustive day of research, little did I know that the morning would bring a revelation. That night, a flash of inspiration struck, my dreams illuminated with a captivating vision that not only piqued my curiosity but also set in motion all the puzzle pieces that were would soon align seamlessly.

Seeing it in a dream may sound cliché, I'll admit, and many may harbor skepticism about the power of the law of attraction.

However, I've always embraced this philosophy throughout my life, allowing it to help guide me towards reaching my goals. I've made it an integral part of daily life, sharing its essence with my daughters and mentees whenever possible. I hold a strong belief that the daily environment we immerse ourselves in helps shapes our life's outcomes. Entrepreneurship isn't something that merely falls into your lap; it's a pursuit that demands active seeking, nurturing, time, and investment. Anyone can dream, but it's commitment that paves the path to success. Think of it as planting the seed of entrepreneurship; without consistent care, exposure to sunlight, and nourishment, it will not grow.

Returning to that pivotal night that would change the course of my journey, I vividly remember the dream. I entered a youth center, filled with young women navigating their own unique set of challenges. My attention was drawn to a particular young woman with whom I struck up a conversation. She shared that she was eager to learn how to start a business so that she can become self-reliant. She exuded brilliance and positive energy, yet she faced significant barriers due to her circumstances.

I awoke with a sense of unease.

The following day, I attempted to shake off the feeling, but then something ironic occurred—a rebound effect. It's akin to when you're told not to think about a red car, and suddenly, all you notice are red cars. It's the notion that once a thought takes hold, it's challenging to erase. I interpreted this as a sign and allowed my thoughts to flow freely.

> **"Just when the caterpillar thought the world was over, it became a butterfly."**
>
> – Unknown

CHAPTER 9: THE PERFECT STORM

Once more, I stood at a crucial crossroads in my life, and in that pivotal moment, I chose the path of wonderment. It was this very choice that gave birth to ShePreneur.

ShePreneur collaborates closely with partners to deliver intensive ten-week entrepreneurial workshops, followed by mentoring and microfinancing programs. Our mission is to provide knowledge and instill a fresh, motivated mindset in women who have entrepreneurial dreams but require guidance to turn them into reality. To launch, we forged a partnership with Toronto Metropolitan University (TMU) to develop a tailored curriculum and The Starfish Foundation in Manhattan, New York, which facilitated connections with women's organizations eager to engage with our programs.

During our first year, our primary focus was on women who stood to gain the most from our program—individuals who encountered significant barriers. Twenty-seven resilient women joined our pilot program, most of whom had faced dire circumstances and found themselves in situations where they demanded a fresh start. Some had experienced the harrowing ordeal of human trafficking at a young age but were determined to forge a brighter future. What united all these women was their shared aspiration to embark on a new journey and seek self-reliance and self-sufficiency through entrepreneurship, a path that would enable them to design the lives they envisioned.

After weeks of training and successfully completing the program, these women emerged better equipped with both business acumen and business plans. The businesses they established spanned a diverse spectrum, from accessory stores and jewellry boutiques to farmers' markets and catering. The culmination of their journey was an exhilarating pitch session, where they presented their business ideas to a panel, competing for startup funding. Understanding the challenges they had overcome made their achievements all the more inspiring.

Each graduate of ShePreneur emerges ready to start their entrepreneurial journey. What's even more impactful is the potential of these businesses to serve their communities by offering solutions and resources, stimulating local economies, and ultimately creating employment opportunities. These women-led ventures possess the power to initiate significant socioeconomic changes in their respective communities.

When ShePreneur first came to me in a dream, I could hardly fathom the potential it held. It was during the graduation ceremony in Mexico City for our pioneering group of women that I was truly struck by the transformative power of our program. I was so moved by the smiles on their faces that were filled with pride, accomplishment, and hope for their newfound futures.

I am overjoyed to announce that our programs not only impart valuable skills and guidance but also instill confidence in women, setting them on a path towards empowerment.

What lies ahead? ShePreneur is shifting to transition into a social enterprise, harnessing its revenue streams to catalyze profound social change on a global scale. Our commitment remains: to champion female entrepreneurship in every facet.

Our mission is to fuel the entrepreneurial spirit in women, providing them with guidance and access to the essential resources required for creating successful businesses. To achieve this vision, we are actively formulating plans to introduce five dynamic channels within the ShePreneur platform: encompassing media, a marketplace, financing solutions, resource hubs, and a thriving entrepreneurial ecosystem.

CHAPTER 9: THE PERFECT STORM

I stand on the threshold of an exiting future for ShePreneur. Through this journey, I've not only quenched my thirst for novelty but also reignited the flames of my entrepreneurial passion. My creative juices are flowing once more, and, above all, I find myself channeling my energy towards a purpose that truly nourishes my soul.

The storm will invariably attempt to engulf you, tempting you to surrender and be carried away. However, if you can resist this and persevere, it often steers you towards uncharted horizons, potentially leading you to a new island waiting to be unveiled — an island with hidden treasures, perhaps even undiscovered diamonds!

With the clarity of hindsight, I now see that after weathering the perfect storm, I am left with an overwhelming sense of optimism and gratitude. My newfound island represented another chance in the world of entrepreneurship.

ShePreneur emerged as the vibrant rainbow after the storm.

From me to you

Write these words down on a piece of paper, fold it up, and always keep it handy. Let intuition guide you and open it only when the moment truly resonates.

"The magnitude of the crisis paves the way for extraordinary opportunities."

– **Tanya**

A Tale from the Sea

Alana Kayfetz
Founder and CEO, Mom Halo

> **"I met myself for the first time, in motherhood."**
> –Beyoncé

I run an online and in-person community called Mom Halo, designed for millennial moms. We offer value and insight into the daily grind of parenthood, and give moms a great day every day, with educational and inspiring content. I went from hosting events in my living room to growing to nearly twenty-five thousand followers on Instagram and raising nearly two hundred thousand dollars for sick kids in under a year.

I got a taste of making money for myself at a very young age. I loved the freedom and power it allowed me.

My Work Ethic

I grew up in a family business and started filing documents in my dad's law practice at eight years old. The desire to work and contribute to the betterment of my family was ingrained in me.

In grade nine, I got an after-school job on a retail floor at a well-known store in downtown Toronto. I worked ten hours a week for nearly four years, raking in top commissions for selling before I was fourteen years old. By age fifteen, I started off the school year by selling wholesale chocolate bars from my locker to afford myself the chance to travel abroad. By eighteen years old, I had started a babysitting company. I was making so much money that my parents were scared I was not going to go to university.

However, it wasn't until I became a mother that I leaned into becoming a full-fledged entrepreneur. I was already well on my way to creating a high six-figure business, with my goals set on breaking seven figures. I just needed to endure. This is the perfect storm. There are no straight lines in this story. It was the ultimate life-changing experience of motherhood that brought me to the most complete version of myself.

THE BOOB STRUGGLE

Boobs.

It has always been an area of my body that has brought me joy, judgment, conversation, fun, and struggle. They were my sex appeal. They were my shame. They were my favourite body part. They were my least favourite body part. Sometimes I would hide them under a turtleneck or a baggy hoodie. When it suited me, I would wear low-cut tops, or use my breasts for power.

Sometimes I really loved my breasts, and sometimes I really hated them. There was no time more evident than in later life when I became a mother. I had a very hard time breastfeeding. All of a sudden, I had to feed a human with them! And after being pregnant for the first time, my boobs were a massive mess.

In the moments after my first entry into motherhood, I thought I was done, my goose was cooked! I was never coming back to life, as I was hit with the Mack truck of early motherhood. I had the most false expectation of myself in motherhood.

Like many millennial moms, I spent my days pregnant, taking selfies of my outfits and my bump. I spent hours researching strollers and not truly focusing on the things that I now know would have benefitted from some time and research. If I had been given any piece of advice, it would have been to watch as many breastfeeding videos as possible. Cause damn, it was a struggle. But in the struggle, I met myself for the first time in motherhood. This nursing journey was the catalyst for my adventures in the entrepreneur ecosystem. Like so many business ventures, my business baby was birthed from a mom of real struggle.

It took twenty-one days to get a good breastfeeding latch with Elias (my firstborn). I wanted to give up every single day. It hurt so much. I could never get the hold right—he was losing weight, and I was sleepless and losing my mind. My breasts suddenly, once sexualized and revered, were now milk makers.

It was not until I tried nursing my baby in public for the first time and felt so much shame and discomfort, that I knew there had to be a place, time, and space for moms to nurture their babies and nourish themselves comfortably.

Elias was six months old when I felt truly comfortable with him at the boob. It was in those moments I was seeking a community of moms. At that moment, in a hip restaurant on Queen Street West in Toronto, it dawned on me.

What if I started hosting high-end events for nursing moms in Toronto's most sought-after restaurants? A place for them to just be themselves, and feel comfortable nursing or bottle feeding or whatever, with the background of something glamorous—wine, food, and friends.

This was the turning point for me, and my struggle to turn my life into the vision of a new community. This was the dawn of my new business venture, and it all happened suddenly and by mistake.

The Takeaway

If you are exploring a passion or are in pursuit of a business venture, I encourage you to answer this question: Have you had a significant moment or a point of struggle that would perhaps could be a foray into a problem-solving venture?

THE STRUGGLE TO RESIGN

I will never forget the day I resigned from my day job. I felt like I had spent my twenties and early thirties working my way up to my director role. It was not until my second maternity leave that I found the courage to take the plunge. I wanted to go all-in on myself, and in order to do so, I had no choice but to leave my nine-to-five.

My husband and I calculated what I would need to bring home monthly, and the bare minimum to maintain our lifestyle. What would be required for me to leave my job and what was realistic for me to earn and pay myself in my pursuit to be my own boss?

Three thousand dollars a month. That was all I had to make to ensure we were okay.

It was at this moment that I decided I would never work for someone else ever again. Leaving my job meant I was really doing this thing. I was going to believe in myself and my ability to earn and lead a company.

How could I show up for my day job, my side hustle, and my kids? I did not have enough hours in the day, and something had to give. The thing I was most excited about was my business. I could not let my family slip, so the only obvious choice was to step into my full self and do what I loved.

I resigned that day, making one hundred thousand dollars a year from my employer.

By the fall of 2020, my business had declared a revenue of $266,000. I had worked half as hard, being way more accessible for my kids and family life, and my revenue had doubled in one year.

The moral of the story is: put pen to paper and make a list of what you must earn. Once it's penned out, you may see that it's not that scary. You might realize that you can fully engage in your true calling. Take a dip, and set sail toward the vision of your dream island.

THE SICK KIDS STRUGGLE

Nothing could have prepared me for having a sick kid. Of all of the storms I have endured and of all the ships I had ever sailed, this one was the hardest to captain by far.

Allow me to illustrate the harsh reality of coping with the news of a child's illness.

December 2020:

I am well on my way into growing a six-figure company while raising two kiddos and learning that we were expecting a third child. While not planned, we were happy about this new family growth. We announced our pregnancy and were excited about and nervous about having three kiddos under four.

March 2020:

I was five months pregnant when the pandemic started. Not only did we have to pivot our life, like so many did, but the basis of what our company was founded on was halted. The lifeblood of our community was live events—meeting and greeting, networking, socializing, educating, and bringing joy to moms. The stress around COVID and what we now know to be the ultimate dawn of a new day shifted everything. During the start of the pandemic and for all of 2020, my goal was to keep my company alive. I was not going down on that ship. Luckily, we had a committed online community. This was the saving grace that allowed me to scrape along that year, all while managing a two-year-old and a four-year-old, while a new baby was on the way.

Henry was born in July 2020. Like my other kiddos, he was born at home with the guidance of a midwife. He did not look like my other kids. In fact, he looked like no one I had ever seen. I have footage of me alone with him in those early days remarking out loud, "Who the heck do you look like, kid?"

At his three-month check-up (which took place when he was nearly four months old), my pediatrician told me she heard a heart murmur. Little did I know, this was the beginning of the complexities we now face. By the time Henry was five-and-a-half months old, he had already had two heart surgeries. We lived at SickKids from November of 2020 until March of 2021.

One day, while I was pacing the halls, I saw a mom crying in the hallway. Once I noticed her, it was impossible not to notice all of the hardness and sadness we parents and caregiver folk were experiencing. Everywhere I looked, I saw sadness. My older kiddos needed me — my partner needed me. Everyone needed me, and I was sinking to depths I had never experienced before. The business basically was handed over to my team at the time to run, as I was completely unavailable for daily operations.

It was at this moment, the hardest of my life and as a parent, that I decided to commit to acts of radical generosity. This was my way of coping with my new reality. To cope with my deep personal loss and stress, I threw myself completely into a vortex of protection. I had to protect my kids, my business, and myself.

I launched a new company rebrand. In the rebrand and restructure, the business is committed to acts of kindness and generosity. This is executed through charitable giving, and the current cause that's close to my heart is SickKids, The Hospital for Sick Children in Toronto.

On the heels of our recovery, we got a call from our genetics team at SickKids. They wanted to meet to discuss a finding.

On April 1, 2021, we learned that our son has an extremely rare condition called Myhre Syndrome. He is one of under two hundred people in the world with it, making him one in 38 million. It's a completely random mutation that creates a variety of lifelong physical and developmental challenges. My life was forever changed. I did not know how we would manage — three kids under five, one now with a rare genetic syndrome with little research and lots of issues. A business I was so desperately attempting to keep afloat.

It was too much for me to handle. At that moment, I was ready to toss in the towel. I was ready to resign from my life, my business, and all that I had ever come to know because I could not imagine how I would be able to manage it all.

But it was also in that moment, in the darkest deep dive of my reality, that I saw the light. You have no idea how strong you are until you have no choice but to be that strength.

The Takeaway

Struggle creates resilience. Do not shy away from hard. As Glennon Doyle says, we can do hard things. Turn the ship around. Enduring moments on the rough seas are the battlefield of our life's work and journey. As moms and as business owners, we cannot pick the other route. We cannot lock ourselves in our bathroom and cry on the floor for days. We get minutes, and then we have to pick ourselves up and move on.

The ship must sail toward the horizon, and we must captain it. No matter the tide, the wind speed, the height of the waves and how hard they crash down, we cannot let a shipwreck occur.

But then it does. When we sink, and the ship's mast is the only thing left, it's our feminine divine energy, our universal truth, and the spirit and vibe of our life's work that bring us back to the surface. Perhaps the better concluding analogy is this: we are not just any little sailing ship. This is not your average vessel. We are the goddamned ark. Like Noah's ark, charged with giant responsibilities to a microcosm of stakeholders.

So think big.

Change the world.

Live your wildest dreams.

And lean hard toward the struggle. Fail a lot, and then make a list from those million-dollar failures.

From Me to You:

We are like Noah's ark, and the eye of the storm is upon us. We will survive, one way or another. But the question is, which oar will we choose to help guide us toward the lighthouse of our future lives and future selves?

– Alana

CHAPTER 10:
THE OTHER BOATS

Having run a communications firm for nearly two decades, I've had the privilege of collaborating with a diverse set of businesses and CEOs. Our typical client profile primarily encompassed small to medium-sized enterprises, and we remained loyal in our support until they reached the point where they could take on their communications internally.

In the early stages of our partnerships with these clients, the playing field was fairly level. A common thread united them – a shared ambition to bolster brand awareness, enhance their financial performance, and nurture sustainable growth. We were fortunate, as the majority of our clients maintained strong relationships with us that spanned many years. This longevity allowed us a unique vantage point from which we could witness their remarkable growth and celebrate their accomplishments.

Using a consistent approach with all new clients year after year, I began to unravel an intriguing pattern. Among our clients, there was sometimes a stark contrast in their growth trajectories; some achieved remarkable success, exceeding even our highest expectations, while others grappled with challenges, some even struggling to meet financial obligations after years. It's worth noting that all these businesses were fueled by a strong determination to prosper, and they possessed robust business models, which is why we chose to collaborate with them in the first place.

So, what set these two groups apart? Remember that initially, they all started out around the same level. Certainly, there are numerous contributing factors to consider, such as value proposition, growth strategy, industry dynamics, innovation, available resources, funding, and more. However, what caught my attention was a distinctive and crucial aspect: the mindset of the CEOs steering these companies. Among those struggling with sluggish growth, there was a common thread. Whenever we convened to assess reports or discuss new strategies their focus was invariably shifted away from their own brand. Instead, they fixated on their competitors, harbouring envy towards their accomplishments. They pondered how and why these rivals were thriving and, in some instances, even contemplated directly copying their strategies. It's worth emphasizing that there are undeniable advantages to conducting competitive audits, a practice we routinely employed when creating strategies for our clients. However, it is imperative that these assessments stem from a constructive perspective.

Alternatively, during the meetings with the businesses that experienced rapid and sustained growth, the nature of our conversations took an evident and refreshing turn. Without getting into the details, these discussions revolved around their unique trajectory, rather than fixating on their competitors. The dialogue shifted towards the improvement of their company, future-oriented growth strategies, and the proactive pursuit of their own route to success.

> **"Comparison is the thief of joy."**
> – Roosevelt

CHAPTER 10: THE OTHER BOATS

When it came to the group that faced challenges in establishing themselves, the damaging practice of constantly benchmarking their performance against other businesses, caused these CEOs to lose focus on their trajectory and the potential successes that lay ahead. They found themselves stuck in a black hole of envy, expending precious energy in an unproductive direction that ultimately hindered their progress. Conversely, the successful companies and their CEOs exhibited a different approach. They concentrated on their own journey, focusing on how they could continue to give the best of themselves while staying in their own lane.

In business, it's a given that there will always be companies similar to yours. Many of them may operate within your industry, competing for the same customer base or even offering identical products or services. The key lies in your belief that your offering stands out as superior for your target audience, and this superiority can manifest in various ways, such as a unique selling point, pricing, quality and much more.

To thrive, ensure you have a robust revenue model, maintain a commitment to innovation, prioritize quality, and forge meaningful connections with your customers. Combine these elements with diligent effort and creative marketing strategies, and you're on the right path.

Shift your mindset from constant comparisons with other businesses and don't shy away from something just because someone else is already doing it, instead figure out how to do it better. Focus on optimizing your own business to its fullest potential, irrespective of the competition. Your dedication to becoming the best version of your business will naturally set you apart and lead you toward success.

Instead of Competing, Focus on Creating

As a mother with two daughters, I've observed a common tendency among them: the inclination to compare themselves, both with each other and their friends. Recently, I decided to have a heart-to-heart conversation with them about what I often refer to as one of life's "deadliest poisons" – the act of comparing oneself to others. I emphasized how this habit can lead them down a path of negativity, eroding their confidence and self-worth in many ways.

While it's entirely natural and common to engage in such comparisons, I wanted to convey that, in reality, it defies common sense. Let me illustrate this with a personal example. One day, my daughter Cara came home feeling frustrated because her friend had outperformed her on a math test. Cara believed she should have matched, if not exceeded, her friend's performance. It was in that moment that I sat her down and posed the following questions:

"Did your friend sleep better than you the night before the test?"

"Was her tummy full or empty when writing the test?"

"How many hours did she put into studying for the test?"

"Did she have a tutor to help her or did she study on her own?"

"How was she feeling when she wrote the test?"

"Does she take extra math classes?"

Cara couldn't resist rolling her eyes in her signature sassy fashion and responded with a nonchalant, *"I don't know,"* to every single one of my inquiries. Case in point: referring to a science principle, unless we can meticulously control every variable, how

CHAPTER 10: THE OTHER BOATS

can there ever be fair grounds for comparison? As humans, we often delude ourselves into thinking we can genuinely measure our worth against others, but upon closer examination we realize that this act, unless conducted with scientific rigor (which, let's face it, rarely happens), is fundamentally flawed. Instead, the wisest investment of our time lies in introspection and self-improvement. I am not here to offer the same lesson I gave to Cara, but rather to emphasize that fierce competition in business is inevitable. Fixating on the other ships sailing the same sea will only serve to hinder your progress. There's no need to feel apprehension toward these fellow boats; in fact, their presence signifies safe waters and if there are many of them nearby, you know the fish are plentiful.

My sister-in-law stumbled upon a brilliant business idea and eagerly researched it, only to be saddened by the discovery that someone else had already executed it. At the time, she told my father about this setback, who responded with strong advice, "That's actually perfect! Now you know the business model is viable; your task is to concentrate on how to execute it even more effectively."

When building a business, attitude will be your biggest challenge, and it's this attitude that determines ultimate success. I preach to young business owners that they should strive to master the ability to be adaptable. In life and in business, there will always be a new situation, the next new thing, someone will always have something better than you and will put what you are doing into question. The key is to adapt to the environment, roll with the times, keep your head high and trust in yourself, knowing that you are doing the best you can, always.

Entrepreneurship can be a fierce journey. I've learned that the ones that come out on top have the ability to focus on their own path and their path alone. They embrace their own successes and failures by doing their best and not defining their journey based on others. You will never see what could be unless you throw your whole self at achieving your dream. Imagine how many people could sit at the top one percent if they just focused. Just think about how many beautiful voices there are in the world, but how few make it to the top of the charts?

Look at the abundance around you, it's yours for the asking.

From Me to You:

Don't fall into the trap of defining your life's successes and failures based on comparing yourself to others. It's the things that differentiate us that make us unique and valuable to the rest of the world.

– Tanya

CHAPTER 10: THE OTHER BOATS

A Tale from the Sea

Julie Bednarski
Founder and CEO, Healthy Crunch

Positivity has always been my guiding star. I'm able to see the glass as half full. I can pinpoint the silver lining in the gloomiest of clouds. And when the waves crash in around me, I have the conviction to see through the storm.

Life is like setting our boat out to sail on the vast, open waters. Before venturing out, we take the time to build our boat to the best of our ability so it will stay afloat. We stock it with equipment, tools, and essentials so we're fully prepared. When we push off from the shore, we're free to do with our journey whatever we wish. As we sail along, we find that the weather is always changing, and the sea has unpredictable ebbs and flows. It isn't always smooth sailing, but we can handle it. We can keep travelling forward. We can find the happiness through it all, if we are so willing.

....

I was growing up and preparing to set sail. It wasn't until the age of about twelve that I remember ever taking significant notice of the other boats around me.

Who are those other boats?
Why are they in the same body of water?
What do they look like?
Where are they going?
When will they reach their destination?
How do they manage their belongings onboard?

I was a preteen, overweight, and severely bullied because of it. At that time, I didn't have a voice to stand up for myself; or rather, I didn't know how to use it. I kept gaining weight until one day, I became completely fed up. You might say I arrived at my lowest point—the point where change is inevitable because there is no other way. I had come to a blockade in my sea, where there was a channel to the left and a channel to the right. Which one would I take? Enough was enough. I chose the channel to the right—the one that represented real, significant change.

It was difficult to be bullied, to feel badly about myself, and to see all the other boats forming close-knit friendships and expanding their social lives. Yet while it was anything but an easy time, I didn't dwell there. I knew there was something greater in store for me.

And so, it began. My transformation.

I committed to changing my life habits to get the results I wanted. I began eating healthy and exercising. After one year, I had lost a significant amount of weight. Feeling lighter and better on my feet, I ran my first marathon. Whereas unhealthy foods were a source of comfort before, they served me no longer. I had a new path and a new mission. What I didn't realize at the time was that my new path was headed somewhere unintentional.

The control I now had over my food intake and my weight loss fuelled me to push through all preconceived boundaries. Looking back, I believe I was simply an impressionable child—a preteen in need of a little extra attention. My parents were busy entrepreneurs just trying to make it as two immigrants in this country. They worked a lot, and I was often on my own.

How much weight do I need to lose to get their attention? I would wonder to myself.

CHAPTER 10: THE OTHER BOATS

With food as one of my few sources of control, I kept stretching myself further and further. Skip breakfast, skip lunch, skip dinner … how long could I go without a meal? Exercise became compulsive and obsessive. I challenged myself harder and harder.

I remember reaching a point where I even surprised myself with how thin I had become. By the age of fifteen, I was anorexic. My parents did take notice; however, it didn't match the level of support, love, and concern that I wanted and needed. I saw a therapist a few times, but it wasn't enough to make any lasting change.

There was a fundamental issue at play: my negative behaviours were giving me positive reinforcement. The bullying dissipated and I became more accepted in social circles. So I simply carried on with all my daily rituals behind the scenes. No one was the wiser.

In my twenties, I was still extremely slim, but managing myself just fine. People around me recognized the fact that I was thin, but never suspected that I was engaging in any form of unhealthy behaviour. I finished university and became a registered dietitian.

Seven more years passed without change, and the career path I chose reflected my ongoing drive to find the perfect diet (meanwhile, no such thing exists!). Passionate about nutrition and health, it was a good avenue, and one that just happened to land me my dream job at a plant-based health food and supplement manufacturer. As my career was taking off, my body was finally beginning to feel the repercussions of my actions over the last seventeen years. I lost my period and began to suffer from severe insomnia and exhaustion. Depression, anxiety, hormonal imbalance, and digestive issues plagued me.

Sure, I was aware of the fact that I had a problem. The thing is, when you're deep in the water, you don't always see the situation for what it truly is. It's like looking through rose-coloured glasses.

My anorexic lifestyle was no longer serving me. Quite the opposite, it was negatively affecting my job, my career, and my personal relationships.

Then it happened. I was let go from my job. My boat had come face-to-face with a massive stone wall in the middle of the sea and there was no way around it. I had to face it and then turn around to rebuild my boat and carve out a new channel to set sail.

Utterly devastated, I had reached the next low point in my life. At that time, the other boats in my life were the furthest from my mind. This was about *my boat*, and more importantly, how I was going to make it sail again.

I began by completely re-evaluating every facet of my life. What was I doing? Where was I going? While I couldn't answer all the questions swirling through my head, I knew one thing for certain: This happened for a reason. That full reason is unclear right now, but it won't be for long. This isn't over; I just need to figure a few things out.

What I figured out was that the very first thing I needed to do was heal. I started with medical tests and doctors' appointments. These gave me insight into exactly what was going on in my body that had to be addressed quickly and effectively. I began working with a personal trainer who, quite inadvertently, talked openly with me about what I was going through. It was talk therapy more than it was physical exercise, but it marked a pivotal point in my mission to get my boat back in the water.

CHAPTER 10: THE OTHER BOATS

I realized that in order to give myself a proper chance to truly heal from the inside out, I needed to get away from it all—the noise, the skepticism, the concern, the love, the support, the worry, the judgment, the distractions. I needed to go to a place where no one knew my name. Oh, and preferably that was also warm and peaceful.

Florida.

I packed a suitcase and my two beloved dogs in the car and away I went.

Because my hormone levels were, quite literally, at zero, the very first step in my healing process was to undergo aggressive hormone therapy. This was essential in order to get my menstrual cycle back, and yet it was one of the most difficult aspects of my healing journey because with it came the most extreme weight-gain and weight-loss cycles. For someone suffering from an anorexic mindset, you can imagine how difficult this was.

In Florida, I attended a health retreat and enlisted a doctor who took me through numerous sessions of formal talk therapy. She helped me change the lens through which I viewed myself and my life. She guided me through a transformation in my thought processes around success, happiness, self-worth, weight, appearance, and size. After several months, she told me it was time to go out into the real world—to get a job and reintroduce myself into society. I needed to accept with open arms who I was at that exact point in time, where I was in my healing process, and what size of pants I fit into.

This was a huge moment. A moment where I realized the true power of acceptance. *Full* acceptance. It was a milestone I'll never forget and one that I carry with me to this day. Because being able to accept ourselves is precisely what we need to blur the view of the other boats. During my healing process, it didn't matter what my family thought, whether or not my friends understood what I was going through, or how my neighbours reacted to my weight fluctuations with each passing week. What mattered was that I was healing and that I knew I was on the right path, regardless of what it took. By learning to mentally accept myself each day, I was healing one of the most important components of the body: my mind.

After about nine months in Florida, I felt well enough to return to my home city of Toronto. By that time, I was an average-sized woman on the open waters yet again — this time moving in a healthy direction.

My mom and I have always shared a love for crunchy, crispy foods, and in this new phase, I was determined to find crunchy snacks that packed a healthy punch. That's when kale chips entered my life.

Delicious! And 100 percent guilt-free.

There were just two problems: 1) they were hard to come by in the city, and 2) the ones I could get my hands on weren't quite up to par.

So I started making my own. They were super crunchy and made with only clean ingredients. I ate them myself and fed them to the odd friend and family member. The feedback I received was phenomenal! I shared them with a few more people, then a few more, and then a few more. People *loved* my kale chips.

I began spending time in a community kitchen in the city where I could use professional equipment and make more food items in bigger quantities. The day I bought my first dehydrator I thought I would feed the whole world with my kale chips! (Today

I own twenty-one, and still I don't yet have the full world at my plate.) There I was, starting my own mini kale chip business and becoming my own boss—just what my parents had always instilled in me as a child. I attended local food fairs and various events that enabled me to sell my product. There are no words for the love I had for what I was doing and the joy I experienced seeing people eat my product and feel *good* about what they were putting into their bodies.

Healthy Crunch was born.

My passion for better-for-you foods had finally collided with my health-focused skillset. To this day, my work fulfills me in every way. When my boat came face-to-face with the stone wall and forced me to turn around a few years earlier, *this* is why. I was meant to heal, to grow, to become the best version of myself, and to be the owner of my company.

Every seed of opportunity will blossom when the season is right.

In the beginning, I never said no. I went to every fair, every event, and handed out every free sample bag of kale chips that I possibly could. One day I was at an event in Toronto and a woman approached me to ask for a free sample for her friend. I gave it to her and never thought twice about it. Little did I know that her friend was a prominent executive at Starbucks.

To my delighted surprise, Starbucks contacted me a week later for a meeting about my kale chips. *My* kale chips! As you might imagine, I wasn't even close to being prepared for a meeting as significant as with Starbucks, but I happily attended. They loved my story and my passion for the business, and the VP of Global Procurement asked me, "How many units can you make a month?"

Huh? I have no idea! is what I wanted to say.

My actual answer was, "About one hundred thousand." There was no part of me that knew how I was going to pull off making one hundred thousand bags of kale chips a month, but never say no, right?

I landed the contract. It was time to sail full mast. I exhausted my savings and obtained a business loan in order to purchase a facility, renovate it from top to bottom, design the space, and fill it with all the equipment I needed. I was overextended, but I had the commitment from Starbucks. And it was this contract that gave me the brand awareness and product trust I needed to catapult Healthy Crunch into something real. Everyone was talking about it and I became known as the "kale chip lady" in Starbucks. My brand was quickly elevated and within the first year of opening my facility, I landed distribution with numerous well-known national retail outlets. I was on a roll and it felt great.

Then the blinders came off. The sun was shining above me, the wind was blowing through my hair, and I was sailing along my chosen water path. Every so often, I began to catch myself looking around. There were those other boats again — this time, the boats were my competitors.

I wanted to know who they were, what products they sold, how many SKUs they had, and which stores they were in. There was a tendency for me to compare. Constantly. Being intimately aware of your competition can be frightening, but only if you let it. Sometimes it's easy to get locked in a spiralling downward undertow that feels like it's taking you with it. To be honest, only after several years in business did I fully recognize what I was doing and came to terms with the fact that it wasn't serving me at all.

If there is one thing I've learned in my journey it's that the other boats in your life, be they professional or personal, don't matter nearly as much as you might think. This is because no other boat will ever be *you*.

Constantly comparing your business to those of your competitors will only result in a race you'll never win. The beauty of competition is that every company has something different to offer. We're all on our own journeys, following unique paths. Knowing who the other boats are is one thing, but obsessing over them is quite another. Be aware of them if you like, but stay your own course through the waters.

Adapt and roll with the unpredictable sea that surrounds you. Tomorrow may not look the way you had planned, but remember that everything happens for a reason — even if you can't see it just yet. We all have our storms to get through, and we can't always see the storms other boats are experiencing across the ocean. As we sail along, whatever we're confronted with is what we must face. It might require courage and grit, or compassion and understanding, or dedication and commitment, or perhaps, the wisdom and grace to fully accept it just the way it is.

From Me to You:

The other boats will always be there. The question is, what will you do with them? Will you let them dictate your every move? Or will you acknowledge their existence, accept yours, and continue sailing along the path that can only belong to you?

– Julie

CHAPTER 11:
THE ANCHOR

Dream, Create, Build, Repeat

If you want something to last, it will take time to build. You will have to use the very best materials, workmanship, and continue working on it forever, constantly improving it. I founded several businesses, and each time started out the same. As soon as I had my business idea, I felt the same intense desire to just move faster and faster to put my plan into action. It always felt like a race to the finish line, filled with excitement, passion, and motivation. But every time I tried to hurry a step in the process, I faced the consequences.

It has taken me many years to learn, and if I am being honest, I still haven't quite mastered it. Entrepreneurship is a marathon not a sprint and the joke is on me — there is no real finish line to this race. The sand in your hourglass never stops running as an entrepreneur.

As you run your entrepreneurial marathon, it's important to also take a break. Recalibrate and anchor yourself. Look back on your journey to gain important insights and learnings that you can apply when looking at how to conquer the path ahead.

Think practical, systematic, organized, well planned, and conservative with calculated risks for a stronger outcome. Not the sexy entrepreneur thoughts you would expect? When you are building something that will stand the test of time, you need to think differently. Small and consistent actions will get you there.

I frequently incorporate breaks into my daily routine, primarily with the aim of recentering myself. These breaks hold a significant importance for me as it enables a deeper reflection on my past experiences and how those can be translated into valuable insights for future endeavors. Entrepreneurship has never been a choice for me; it's an inherent part of who I am. I've come to realize that I will continue to embark on new business ventures throughout my life. My passion for the entrepreneurial world is so intense that after selling my business, I decided that I wanted to expose myself to the world of angel investing and joined a local network.

My excitement is genuine when encountering startups and engaging with incredibly enthusiastic entrepreneurs. Amid these fresh opportunities, I recognized the need to personally define the attributes of a successful business that resonate with me. These self-imposed criteria would act as anchors, keeping me firmly grounded when making investment and business decisions, preventing me from being swayed solely by the charisma of an entrepreneur or a captivating business idea. While I acknowledge the pivotal role that numbers play, I also understand the importance of the intangible qualities that a business should possess to be deemed as promising.

To further refine my considerations for future business ventures, I made the decision to collaborate with a business coach. This enabled me to shape my entrepreneurial vision and align it with my core values and goals. Here is what we came up with:

Easily Scalable

The capacity to scale a business is paramount for its ultimate success, allowing it to expand, generate revenue, and effortlessly meet growing demand. I must confess that I encountered significant challenges with one of my previous businesses when it came to implementing a scaling model. We struggled with resource constraints and lacked organizational structure. Although we eventually identified a model, I couldn't help but feel it potentially impeded our growth—a frustrating experience. For any future business endeavors, prioritizing scalability is non-negotiable.

Global Reach

The 2020 pandemic highlighted the demand for global economy. Nowadays, purely local businesses are a rarity. We've come to recognize that virtually all the goods and services we encounter daily possess a global footprint, whether in direct or indirect ways. This global interconnectedness is the path forward. Prioritizing global impact and the potential for international operations is central to my business strategies.

Social Enterprise

Naturally, I have an affinity for businesses that generate revenue, but with an exciting twist. I'm drawn to the concept of pursuing financial success while simultaneously striving for positive social, cultural, community, economic, and environmental outcomes. Imagine there was an idea for a business that not only made a profit but also created a meaningful impact. In its most straightforward form, we recognize that convincing people to part with their money can be challenging. However, if they know that by spending their money it will have a positive impact, they would be more likely to engage. No one will get wealthy without enriching the lives of others.

Operations

I aspire to have the capability to conduct operations from anywhere in the world, ready to seize opportunities as they arise. The intriguing cultural variations in global business practices captivate me. Embracing flexible operations could potentially unlock new avenues for growth, especially considering the wealth of lucrative business networks beyond our local city limits.

Succession

I've been increasingly focused on identifying companies with lasting legacy potential. A simple question I find myself asking is, "Can this business not only survive but also thrive in the absence of its founder(s)?" If the answer leans towards no, it becomes significantly less appealing to me. I gravitate towards businesses that possess a robust structural foundation capable of outlasting their founders, the potential to generate passive income, and the ability to seamlessly incorporate new stakeholders as part of their growth trajectory.

Industry

While industry might not be my primary focus, it remains a significant factor in my considerations. Some sectors naturally hold more promise for the future, while others seem destined to become obsolete. It's no coincidence that I'm inclined towards investing time in companies with the promise of Tesla! As I write this, I do realize that with our constantly evolving world there will be emerging industries that we are yet to discover. Nevertheless, I lean towards sectors showing sustained potential for innovation. Of course, industries resilient to recessions and pandemics certainly add an extra layer of appeal.

As Martin Luther King stated, "You don't have to see the whole staircase; just take the first step." As you shape your business, it's essential to consider the guiding principles that will keep you firmly anchored. I strongly encourage every entrepreneur to craft a personalized list of their non-negotiables. This list should be revisited regularly and adjusted as circumstances evolve, but should always serve as the cornerstone around which your business is built.

When confronted with challenging business decisions, these anchors become invaluable reference points. The inception of entrepreneurship carries profound significance, as it is during this phase that you lay the foundation for future success. These guiding principles will be your compass through the inevitable periods of uncertainty and ambiguity that all entrepreneurs encounter at some point in their journey.

Success leaves a trail of clues. Open your eyes wide and gather as much insight as possible from those who have walked the path before you. Why spend years learning through trial and error when someone with experience can steer you in a matter of weeks? You'll save yourself a great deal of heartache and effort by tapping into the wisdom of others' journeys.

You will always remember the moment your business idea sparked to life, the moment you set sail on your entrepreneurial voyage, your very first client, that initial round of funding, and even your first major setback. In the early stages of your journey, these milestones are etched deeply in your memory, radiating with significance. As your journey progresses, these can sometimes fade into routine, so it's important to celebrate the special moments of your adventure. Frequently look back, gauge the distance you've traveled, record your newfound knowledge, and pivot these learnings into usable strategies as you think about the next leg of your journey. Always relying on your anchors as they meant to keep you from drifting.

With strong anchors, you are free to dream, create, build, and then repeat!

From Me to You:

Always choose action over deliberation.
Make your "one day" into today.

– Tanya

CHAPTER 11: THE ANCHOR

A Tale from the Sea

Lara Frendjian, RHN, CPA,CA
Founding Director, Nutrition Her Way

My journey with both nutrition and business started at a young age. Neither approach to these two areas was perfect, but they led me to where I am today. And for that, I am grateful.

I am a nutritionist helping shape women's lives. I say this because my vision is to help them love their bodies, feel their best, and, in turn, help them change the world. I firmly believe that women are trailblazers. Each person has a special mission for the world. A particular assignment to complete. But we often miss that assignment because we're bogged down trying to survive life. And often that happens because we don't feel well. We are overwhelmed with the stress of life and we're exhausted. How can we be trailblazers when we don't have enough energy to make it through the day? I don't believe we can. And that's what fuels my passion to help them, as well as anchor myself through the ups and downs of my entrepreneurial journey. It's not an easy one, but it's the most rewarding journey I've ever dared to embark upon.

My story with nutrition began at a young age. I wanted to learn how to manipulate my weight. As I entered my adolescent years, I noticed I was heavier than my friends. I also realized they could sip on slushies, eat candy all day, and still be skinny. So, I began dieting at a young age, possibly as early as eleven.

This struggle with food continued into my high school years, which made me consider pursuing a career in nutrition. But as I approached grade 12 and had to decide my path, I went in a completely different direction. One that would give me the financial freedom that I desired. I chose to go into finance and pursue a career as chartered accountant (CPA). After all, I enjoyed it, and I was good at it. I remember scoring perfectly on my accounting tests when all my friends struggled to pass. Somehow, this felt like a logical concept to me. Pursuing the field of finance seemed like the safe path to follow, and a career that would pay me well for my efforts. So off I went to university.

Going into finance partially backed by my desire to eventually run my own company. Since I was a little girl, I had these grand visions of being an entrepreneur. I wasn't sure what that company would be, but I knew that my accounting background would always come in handy. The thought of starting my own business was an exciting dream, but one that was also riddled with fear. This is because I had witnessed my parents' struggles, as my dad unsuccessfully attempted to launch multiple businesses.

But I forged on, and left my thoughts of studying nutrition behind. I dove into my studies and graduated with a business management degree, majoring in accounting and finance. I then wrote and passed the CPA exams and went into public accounting. And while my relationship with food improved over the years, my interest in nutrition never went away. I loved food, enjoyed cooking, and remained passionate about healthy eating. I just naturally gravitated toward fruits and veggies, and eating healthy felt easy for me.

Then something happened that I wasn't expecting. I began to enjoy my work in finance beyond my initial expectations. I helped advise CEOs and GMs to make business decisions and worked with brilliant minds. But I always felt unfulfilled. Something in me kept looking for more. When I was in public accounting, I thought maybe it was because I'm behind the scenes, and that perhaps I needed to work in industrial sector to help businesses grow. So I left public accounting and went into the industrial field. When I got there, I still felt that a hole needed to be filled. I thought that I could gain fulfillment by moving to a smaller company where I could provide more oversight and support growth. So, I shifted yet again and went into an industry that I cared about, working for a long-term care home provider. I really began to connect with the vision of that company. I did some rewarding work to help them improve their level of care, but guess what? Something was still missing. I still wasn't satisfied. I still felt unfulfilled. But I kept working long hours there, and lived through stressful days of year-end closes, mergers, and acquisitions as well as public offerings.

I did everything that I thought I was supposed to be doing. I managed a household, raised two daughters, and cultivated a healthy marriage. And at some point, I realized that I wasn't feeling all that great. I thought it was just my age and life was getting the better of me. After all, I was in my thirties, had two kids, and was trying to juggle it all. I still ate relatively healthy and exercised, but something didn't feel right in my body.

I was tired all the time. I often fell asleep with my kids. I was bloated and had put on some midsection weight. I couldn't go without my afternoon coffee, and my PMS was getting the better of me. I thought all this was normal, by the way. So, I exercised more and tried to eat clean, while managing as best as I could. It wasn't until years later that I realized these experiences were messages from my body, trying to tell me that I needed make some changes.

During that time, my husband was experiencing minor health issues, and we went to see a holistic practitioner. Like me, he was perfectly healthy according to his bloodwork, so we needed an alternate solution. As we addressed my husband's concerns, I decided that I might as well get checked out since I was already there. As I began to address my health and make strategic changes to my food, my interest in nutrition started to peak again.

I began to dream again about working in this field and possibly making a career change. Now, this was a scary thought. I liked my job and enjoyed the comfort it brought our family. But I also knew that as I dreamt about the possibility of studying nutrition, I became more excited. I felt that this could possibly merge my vision of running my own business with my passion for nutrition. Throughout the years, I hadn't lost my thirst for running my own business.

I researched some part-time education options, and I shared my findings with my husband. He was fully supportive of my dream and vision and so I began the journey of working, mothering, and studying part-time. I was so passionate about my vision of starting a private practice and helping women feel their best that juggling it all was a breeze.

I loved everything about nutrition. Like a sponge I absorbed everything that was being presented, and the two years flew by. I graduated with honours and decided that as I worked on growing my practice, I would gradually reduce my work in accounting. I joined a venture capital firm as a part-time controller and started a nutrition practice at a medical practice. I was there for about nine months before I joined a friend who was expanding her Chinese medicine practice. She wanted support from a nutritionist for her patients, so I joined her on a part-time basis. We worked together for a couple of years and more and more I realized that I loved my one-on-one work. But my vision to create an inclusive community for women grew stronger.

CHAPTER 11: THE ANCHOR

Community is such an important value for me. I know firsthand that it's easier to do things with community and support. And health is no different. Creating a community and focusing on harnessing a supportive environment is a critical part of doing something that's hard and new.

That's why moving away from working with my friend was such a difficult choice. And to say that this was a difficult choice is an extreme understatement. It was an emotional rollercoaster ride. I felt like I was letting my friend and an entire team down. I had helped set up the vision she had for this clinic. I had helped us move into a new space. I had joined the management team and said yes to expanding the clinic and one day becoming an investing partner.

I also became painfully aware of how petrifying it could be to branch out on my own. All the fears of following in my father's footsteps and failing as a business owner came to the surface. But I dealt with them. It wasn't an easy admission, but as I became aware of my fears, they had less and less control over me.

As difficult as it was, I knew that I had to remain true to myself and my vision. I hadn't done all this and made all these sacrifices to play small or to silence my vision. So we parted ways, and I continued to see clients online and began developing programs to help women who were in my shoes. Busy women juggling career and family, who were struggling to have enough time in their day to do it all. To prepare food for themselves and their families. To have enough energy to make it through the day. To shed the excess weight that seemed to accumulate with each passing year. To love and care for their bodies without dieting. I didn't want women to just survive anymore, but to thrive so they can accomplish all that they were put here on earth to accomplish.

I now have a system that I help take women through, in both group and individual settings. This system helps them make changes to their health and nutrition in a sustainable way. I help them break habits and patterns that no longer serve them. They develop new habits to make meal prep a cinch, as well as break the cycle of perfectionism that leads them to an all-or-nothing approach to nutrition and exercise. That vicious cycle that has them eating perfectly all day, only to let loose and snack through the night. Or eat perfectly through the week and binge through the weekend. My system brings their body into balance, so they have boundless energy and a thriving metabolism as well as reverse the growing waistline without adhering to a strict diet.

I love what I do. It's truly the most rewarding and challenging adventure of my life. I am now fully on my own and have left my career in finance behind. Entrepreneurship comes with a steep learning curve. Many ups, and many more downs. It's an adventure that isn't meant for the faint of heart. You can't just show up and offer a service. You must fall in love with the problem, know your client, manage your time, prioritize your goals, manage social media, market your brand, and maintain your course. And one more thing. You need an anchor that keeps you going. A purpose greater than yourself, even greater than having a financially successful business. It's funny that many of us view an anchor as something that just grounds us. But my anchor both grounds me and helps propel me forward.

My anchor is threefold.

First, is my vision for helping women feel their best so they can accomplish their greater purpose in life. I know firsthand that when we feel well, we have the capacity to pursue our dreams. And when we do, we are unstoppable and can change the world and make it better than when we found it.

Second, my vision is to use my business to fund a nonprofit organization that helps women in impoverished circumstances stand on their own two feet by running their own businesses.

For many years, I volunteered for an organization that helped rescue trafficked women in Cambodia. They had been sold by their families to sex traffickers to help feed the rest of their family. I learned from that experience that if the mothers in those households had skills and a vision or opportunity to start a business, it would end their poverty and help break the cycle of trafficking. Telling you my story is the beginning of the fulfillment of that vision. And for that, I am grateful.

Finally, what really keeps me going are my two girls. I want to raise strong daughters who know how to stay the course. When I've wanted to give up throughout the years, they've kept me going. I want them to dream, embark on adventures, and overcome any barriers. I can't allow myself to quit because I don't want them to be riddled with fear and quit when life gets tough.

From Me to You:

My word of advice for any entrepreneur or hopeful would be to GO FOR IT! You can do it part-time like I did and find a community who will keep you accountable and support you. And once you're on that path, have your vision handy to help keep you anchored during the ups and downs that come from choosing this journey. I had my vision plastered on my laptop, in my workspace, in my journal. I continuously reminded myself why I was doing this. This helped me stay the course and get to where I am today. And for that, I am forever grateful. Take time to see the dreams ahead, journal, create vision boards, voice memos, and listen to podcasts. Surround yourself with everything you need to be inspired.

– **Lara**

CHAPTER 12:
THE DESTINATION

Do you know your destination?

At any given minute, of any given day, I believe we should know the answer to this question.

Right here, right now, what is your destination?

The answer will change with each journey on which you set sail. Our destination today might not look at all like the destination we had five years ago, nor the one we will have five years from now. Destinations are fluid, like the waters we travel through. They can be altered and changed with purpose according to the weather or current environment we find ourselves in.

Sometimes our destinations encompass different facets of our lives. We might have one destination that involves our children's education and another that sails us toward a healthier and more fulfilling way of living. Other times, a destination may take us on a journey far away during which there will be many other little destinations that we reach as we travel. As long as we know where we're going, we can steer our boats in the right direction.

Think of your own life for a minute. Every part of it is either growing or dying at any single point in time. These parts of your life can be physical, emotional, mental, intellectual, professional, or personal. You're either expanding your career (growing) or you're stagnant (dying). You feel happy and enthusiastic each day (growing) or you're unmotivated and depressed (dying). Your mind is constantly buzzing with new, exciting ideas (growing) or it's empty and deflated (dying).

It's anything but easy, but no matter your age, the ultimate goal ought to be feeling as though you are growing in all facets of your life. When you feel dispirited and deteriorated, figure out what's slowing you down and holding you back. Get rid of it because it's no longer serving you. Determine where you want to go next, map out the route, and travel toward it on your new path of purpose, development, and growth.

When I reflect on my time in journalism many years ago, I realize it was a destination never quite reached in its entirety. There I was, with a full-time on-air position, hosting a show that aired nationally across Canada. I loved my career and was slowly realizing that I was ready to grow it even further, in a bigger market with more opportunity—United States here I come!

Knowing this might be one of the biggest moves I would ever make in my life, I thought it would be smart to test the waters first. I went after and landed a contract position that was stationed in Manhattan, New York, on a national and very well-known talk show where I worked for several months. From sitting in production meetings and providing new show ideas, right through to walking the floor during live tapings, I managed the on-air guests and ensured the show went on without a hitch. I was in the heart of it. And I fell in love.

CHAPTER 12: THE DESTINATION

My move to the US was right and I was going to move forward.

I spent weeks throughout the summer cutting the perfect demo tape, refining my résumé and putting together a cover letter that would be part of an amazing package to show off my skills and make me stand out. Everything was ready and all my accumulated efforts were about to be put to the test. The packages would be on the desks of numerous executive producers at all the top broadcast stations across the United States in no time. But then …

BANG!

My father fell ill, and we received the most terrible news. He was diagnosed with a brain tumour and was given one year to live.

No packages were sent. Demo tapes were set aside. Résumés were left sitting to collect dust. I needed to be with my dad. The next year was going to be a treacherous uphill battle and I wanted to be by his side just as he was always by mine.

Needless to say, my career took a fateful twist. That crystal-clear destination of mine had to change. I chose to be close to my father and my family, and I needed flexibility in my work and my life. Mark and I were engaged to be married in September of the following year, but after a heartbreaking meeting with my father's oncologist, we made the important decision to move our wedding date up so that my father could attend. Imagine planning an entire wedding for 250 people in three months, while witnessing your father fall more ill and working through the thought of his death. My father meant the world to me, and this journey was one of the most difficult. However, witnessing his daughter's wedding filled him with immense joy and a sense of peace. For me, having him present and seeing him smile was the best gift of all.

We made it through the most difficult year. He passed surrounded by his most beloved people, and I wouldn't have had it any other way.

After a long pause from my career in broadcasting and the passing of my dad, who also happened to be my biggest cheerleader and source of motivation, I just didn't have the same appetite to get back into it. Instead, my newly found angel pushed me toward a new path in entrepreneurship and that's when I founded my first business.

But my journalism career was still a chapter without an ending. Fast forward almost twenty years and as I found myself digging and soul searching, I realized there was an unfinished voyage to a known destination. Television was calling my name once more. Her voice was loud, repetitive, and relentless.

I made it my destination yet again. The idea of hopping back in wasn't so simple, however. My old tapes and cover letters were now nothing more than fire kindling and it felt as though it had been eons since I was on-air. The way I see it, I had two choices: 1) go after it, or 2) always wonder what could have been.

This is a debate we are faced with often throughout our lives. Are we up on our feet, moving, shifting, finding our way? Or are we sitting back, pausing, delaying, and hoping for the best? In my case, I could have been complacent with my feelings of loss and hopelessness surrounding the tremendous changes that the industry had undergone since I was a part of it so many years ago. Or I could begin learning, researching, sending messages, making phone calls, and rekindling my old connections.

No matter what it is, you'll always find me climbing and being proactive. One move after another, I'm heading to my destination. I'm never stagnant, and never giving up. And I know

CHAPTER 12: THE DESTINATION

every action I take gets me that much closer to reaching my goal. Staying at the bottom of the ladder, looking up hopeful, is not my style. I have never been the type to lack action and initiative to get to my destination or simply stand and wait to be lifted up the rungs.

Part of being proactive is visualizing what you want and where you want to go. Each time you start your engine, set sail out onto the waters, and steer in new directions, you're doing it with your end vision in mind. And because your destination is always there for you to see and imagine wholeheartedly, whether you realize it or not, you're manifesting and attracting it. Step by step, rung by rung, wave by wave, it's getting closer.

After knowing, visualizing, and following my destination once again, it's taking shape. Better equipped, I can now pair my broadcast experience with my entrepreneurial experience. Even though I don't know exactly what it will look like when I'm fully there, I know precisely what my destination is. But the path is still a journey, and I'm reminded that we only need to see the island, we don't need to know what's on it. The treasures buried deep in the sand are for us to discover once we arrive.

As you follow along on your journey, there may be multiple stops. Mini destinations at various intervals may slowly lead you to your final destination. And even then, once you arrive, you may find that it pulls you in a new direction, only to be yet another stop in your journey. Whatever your destination, whatever your plans, whatever your voyage looks like, stay on it. Keep moving toward it. Expect a few bumps and sharp turns, and don't be surprised if you hit a storm or two. It wouldn't be a journey without them. Everything in this life worth having calls for vision, passion, hard work, and dedication.

Carry on.
Push forward.
Trust in your destination until you reach it.

From Me to You:

Will you keep your hands on the wheel and steer your boat to the destination you choose, or will you let your boat drive you to a destination of its choice?

Go with the thought gives you inner peace.

— Tanya

CHAPTER 12: THE DESTINATION

A Tale from the Sea

Tia Slightham
Founder and Parenting Coach, Tia Slightham — Parenting Solutions Inc.

Starting something new, changing directions, and reaching for a different destination can feel scary with all the unknown waters that lie ahead. Where you're heading can often feel away, out of reach, or too difficult to continue, but the truth is you've already reached your destination. Any destination you set forth to reach is yours. Now, you simply need to believe you're there!

Starting my own business and being an entrepreneur isn't exactly what I had in mind, although when I really think about it, I don't know that I had any idea what to expect. What I thought I knew about being an entrepreneur were the ideas around having freedom both financially and in time. I would work from home, be my own boss, and make all the rules!

This all sounds amazing, right?

These are the main reasons many of us strive to become entrepreneurs, and I'm guessing they're partly what's driving you as well. These were the driving factors as I built my business, and continue to be what makes being an entrepreneur a positive experience for me and my family. When I began heading to my destination, I didn't even know that I was on this journey; in fact, it all sort of just happened.

I started as a kindergarten teacher with a master's degree in early childhood education. I had a plan, or at least I thought I did. I graduated, had my own classroom, and at that moment in time, I never thought I would do anything else. I absolutely loved my students and having the opportunity to help them create a positive school experience. I realize now as I look back that even if you think you have a plan ... plans change.

Fast forward fifteen years. I'm no longer teaching kindergarten students; rather, I'm now teaching parents as a positive discipline parenting coach. I moved from the United States to Canada, married my amazing husband, have two of the most incredible boys and am the founder of Tia Slightham — Parenting Solutions Inc. We are a team of four and together we work globally with parents from around the world to help them break the cycle of generational trauma through my coaching program, The Parenting With Purpose Method. We teach parents the skills they need to be the best parents they can be, all while building positive relationships with their kids.

Who would have ever thought that all the paths on my journey would have led me here? With each step I walked, each mile I ran, and every hardship I faced, I have arrived at this destination, but it won't be my final destination. We are continually growing and evolving and that's what makes this journey so incredible. Today I am a strong woman, an entrepreneur, and a six-figure business owner, which all started in the classroom.

This might all feel out of reach and you might be saying to yourself, "No way will this happen to me. I can't do these kinds of things. These are things that happen to other people."

But I'm telling you to stop right there!

I used to think this way too. I 100 percent know where you're coming from. You might have had times where you tried and failed. So did I. Maybe you had ideas that didn't come to fruition. So did I. Someone might have told you that you're not good enough. I know how that feels. But, I want you to know that you get to choose. You get to choose to have it all if you want it. You have all the power and it all stems from within. There's one core part of who you are which will control your outcomes, and it's your mindset.

Mindset is the most powerful thing you own. It drives your ship, steers your boat, and guides you to your destinations. Mindset allows you to keep going when things feel like they're too much to bear. Let me ask you a couple of questions:

Do you truly believe and feel that you can accomplish anything you put your mind to?

Do you think you're capable?

Do you know that you're a superstar?

If you feel nervous reading these statements and it makes you uncomfortable in your own skin, then this is where you must put in the work. The rest falls into place once you allow your mindset to lead the way. I once looked at other people and what they'd accomplished and never believed in a million years that I could have that. But what I now know is that in order to reach my goals, I absolutely must believe in myself from my deepest core. It's not always easy and it takes work, but self-love, self-care, and knowing that you're worthy will lead you to the greatest places. Your mindset will allow you to reach destinations you never thought possible.

People may tell you that you're crazy or make you feel like your ideas are far-fetched or unattainable. Don't let them. You may lie in bed at night second-guessing yourself, trying to self-sabotage and talk yourself out of it. Don't do it. There may be days that feel too hard and make you feel like staying down, not getting back up. Don't allow this. Get up, do you, continue onward toward your destination, and when you look back at where you started you will shock yourself with your strength, determination, and accomplishments.

Guidance is something I desperately needed and continue to need as I grow and reach for bigger goals. Allowing others to help you and being coachable will be critical in your success. You don't need to do this alone. To help you get started, I'm going to share with you three things I do daily that help me stay on course. As you build your business and reach for your dreams I invite you to join me.

1. **Write your top goal down every single day.** Remember this: goals that haven't been set, can't be met! Make your goal something that feels so far out of reach that you almost can't put it down on paper. Let your stomach feel unsettled and your body feel full of nerves. This is how you know you've set your goal appropriately.

2. **Carry your goals with you**. Fold it up in your pocket every day and read it, say it, repeat it. The more you say your goals out loud, the more your mindset will shift and allow you to fully believe in them. Remember, you can accomplish anything that you want to accomplish! It's already yours! Mindset is the key to your dreams becoming your reality.

3. **Take action.** Oftentimes we know what we want to do or goals we want to meet, but we don't take action. In order for you to reach your destination you absolutely must "DO!" Taking action will allow you to make mistakes and have moments of failure. It's during these times where growth

occurs. Growth only happens when you take action toward your desires and goals. Sitting in your fears and not moving forward won't allow you to reach your destination.

Are you ready to do these three simple things each and every day as you move toward your destination? If you have a burning desire and know with your entire being, inside and out, that you can and will reach your goals, then they're already yours. You're there! You've got this and I've got you!

All of this to say, you may not always know exactly where you're headed, but you must keep moving forward. Plans change, the waters shift, your direction may swerve, but if you continue to believe, set your goals and take action on all your amazing ideas, the possibilities are endless. I still work on all of these things myself. The truth is, it's something we all need to do continually. If you're not moving forward with new ideas and growth, you're actually going backward.

From Me to You:

Keep looking ahead to your planned destination. You'll come across speed bumps, hurdles, mountains, and valleys as you trek this journey. Mistakes and times of failure will happen. These are all part of your plan. You can't have ups without downs. You can't have highs without lows. When you feel like giving up, don't. When you feel like you're not good enough, remember that you are. When your goals feel out of reach, reach higher. Remember, you can do anything you put your mind to, and each step you take is the right step toward your destination. Don't wait. Your time is now!

– Tia

CONCLUSION:
TIME TO SET SAIL

There she goes. Bobbing, drifting, coasting in the sea. Her engine hums, her propeller spins, her sails flap in the breeze.

Beautiful. Confident. Ready.

It's time to set sail.

Where is your boat headed?

Perhaps you are destined for the tropical island to the west or the cooler climates of the north seas. Or maybe you're on your way to a faraway land not quite in your line of sight yet.

These are all destinations. Different and unique, but destinations nonetheless. As we have seen with all the women featured in this book, a journey can be long, taking up a lot of time, determination, and hard work before we reach it. It can also be small and quickly attainable, representing a mini milestone on our way to some bigger feat.

Wherever we're headed, today, tomorrow, or next year, when we know what it is we are after, we have a map and a purpose. We move in the direction we want to go. We know where our boat is headed and we drive, steer, and glide our way through the waters until we arrive.

Of course, there may be times when we feel like we lose that sense of direction. Perhaps we can no longer see our destination, or we're not quite sure where our boat is headed anymore. There's nothing wrong with losing our way. It might even help us find a new way — a better way. In these times, it's the searching, map-questing and never-giving-up-attitude that counts.

Knowing where our boat is headed is half the battle of living a happy, successful, and fulfilling life. The second half is being fierce until we reach it. No complacency, no backing down. It's full force ahead.

Remember that you and only you are the captain of your boat. Follow your gut, trust your instincts, and drive. When there are moments where you falter and your boat stands still, or you cross the intimidating high seas, pick yourself up, visualize your end goal, and turn your engine back on. Hear its mighty growl as you prepare to set sail yet again.

As your boat moves through the water before you, its energy creates your wake once more. Watch in wonderment as your wake is sustained and continuous, rippling through the water as far as your eyes can see. Know and trust in the mark you are making on this earth. Watch your own wake, create your own impact, and extend your own ripple through the world.

On your journey, you have a compass. It's within you. Whenever you feel lost, discouraged, doubtful, or unsure, listen to your inner compass. Let it guide you. Once you make the call, don't bother looking back — only forward. Stand tall, breathe deep, take the helm, and steer. This is your boat and your life. At the helm, remember that taking charge isn't only about steering, but also about watching your surroundings. See the weather, take note of the sea's current, and pay attention to the waters around you. Sometimes you'll need to stand up and push your way through, and other times you'll need to sit back and go with the flow. Learn the difference.

There will be high tides and low tides. Moments of glory and minutes of doom. Times when you're floating blissfully and days when it feels like you're sinking deep. Carry on. Be determined and unapologetic in your journey. Find your tools and use them. Pull out your telescope often and remind yourself of where you're headed. Rediscover your destination through the telescope lens and see your vision. We all need a little reminder every now and then — a fresh inspiration to follow our dream, or a motivational jolt to go after what we really want.

You don't need to go at it alone; in fact, you shouldn't. The crew you choose to join you on your journey is just as important as the captain. Select wisely. Surround yourself with people who believe in you and your goals. And then work happily and tirelessly together to get there.

Should you pass through a storm, have no fear. Trust in the strength of your boat, the talent of your crew, the tools you brought along and the vision of the captain: YOU. Without the storm, the stillness would never feel as peaceful. You're not alone. There are many other boats in the waters all around you, and while they can offer comfort, remember to stay focused on your journey. The other boats are not the same as yours — your boat is one of a kind and always will be. There is no need to compare or worry about what they're doing or how fast they're getting somewhere. This is about *your* boat.

Stay the course. Use your anchor for stability. You can always drop it down when you need to reassess your travels. Take time to think about why you set sail in the first place. Sit in your boat. Remember how far you've come and how far you'll still go. Feel good about where you are right now, and even better, about where your boat is headed.

Then, hoist your anchor up again and resume.

Your next destination awaits you.

ACKNOWLEDGEMENT:

Thank you to the incredibly remarkable twelve women showcased in this book. I extend my heartfelt gratitude for your patience, unwavering support, and boundless enthusiasm for this project. It is your invaluable contributions that have truly shaped the essence of this book.

ABOUT THE AUTHOR

Tanya Dodaro is a television host, serial entrepreneur, branding and communications consultant. For twenty years, she has helped emerging businesses and international executives grow their brands and boost their revenues. Her work is founded on three fundamental principles: the pursuit of innovation, a commitment to elevation, and a dedication to disrupting the status quo.

Tanya actively mentors and provides strategic counsel to entrepreneurs through her affiliations with FuturePreneur Canada, venture capital firms and The Forge business incubator at McMaster University. Tanya is the founder of ShePreneur, an online platform committed to empowering and supporting female founders.

Website: tanyadodaro.com

Instagram: @tanya.dodaro

www.ingramcontent.com/pod-product-compliance
Lightning Source LLC
Chambersburg PA
CBHW030938180526
45163CB00002B/609